War Torn:
A Family Story

To Monsoon
with Love

Felicity Vaughan Swayze

Enjoy!

Felicity

May 2018
NYC

ISBN: 1540862232
ISBN 13: 9781540862235
Library of Congress Control Number: 2016920322
CreateSpace Independent Publishing Platform
North Charleston, South Carolina

To Hold in Memory
My Mother, My Father, My Brother

Table of Contents

Acknowledgment

JOE MEDLICOTT, MY STEADY MUSE, I could never have made this journey without you. For your wisdom, patience, constant encouragement, for the countless hours you spent "strafing" my pages. My gratitude knows no bounds.

Preface

PASSPORT ISSUED BY FOREIGN OFFICE, London, 9 August 1940 to Mrs. L. Vaughan. Exit Permit #318701, valid for departure on or before October 9, 1940. Good for one journey only, traveling to Canada and the United States of America. Accompanied by two children. Non Immigrant Visa #1417. August 9, 1940. American Consul General, London, England to Lilian and Peter and Felicity Vaughan. Embarked 10 August 1940. Stamped by the Immigration Officer Glasgow. Admitted August 23, 1940 Halifax, Nova Scotia.

The photograph of the bearer, my mother, 26 years old. She looks more like 15. Her hair is parted in the middle, pulled up behind her ears and then falls to her shoulders. Hair brown, eyes blue. Dress, checked. Buttons covered to match. Sleeves, short. Brooch silver. I search her face, looking for clues. Is she frightened? I see a certain dignity there. But it is all guess work. Is Tom, my father, with her? Is he trying to convince her that this is the right thing to do? Perhaps he is telling her that it is necessary for the children's sake. It is all happening so fast.

It is the summer of 1940 and our world has become seriously disturbed.

Part I

CHAPTER 1

Upheaval

I WAS BORN INTO A world preparing for war. My brother, Peter, and I greeted our parents in the birthing area of the Racliffe Infirmary in Oxford, in
December of 1937. Peter comes first, in usual head down fashion. An hour
later, after giving my mother much grief, I enter this life feet first. I am
definitely here, in spite of my mother's protestations to the doctor and nurses
that there could not possibly be another one in there. We are tiny, less than
five pounds apiece, and spend two weeks in an incubator. We go home to
Lyndworth Close where all baby items have been multiplied times two, for I
have not been expected.

In the larger world, however, most eyes are not on us, as surprising and delightful as we are. The aggressions of Nazi Germany have become the main
event. Our country, Great Britain, is preparing for the time when war may
become the only choice. By 1937, the year of our birth, radar installations
are already operating secretly on the British East Coast. The Royal Air Force
is rearming. Fighter Command, formed in 1938, is developing fighter aircraft
and training young men to fly them. Morris Motors, where my father works,
has been reorganized for war production. He is laid off and can be rehired if
he will take a job on the production line making Spitfire aircraft. He refuses
but somehow manages to stay on, now working in the Service department.

We are war-ready at our house. Nearly 40 million gas masks have been
issued to British civilians as early as 1938. My mother carries three on every
excursion out of the house--one for herself and two for us. Does she throw them
into the double pram or hook them over her arm, carrying her handbag with

the other hand? Are they ugly and frightening looking things? Mrs. Miniver, in the novel by Jan Struthers, takes her children to be fitted, as my mother must have done. Mrs. Miniver describes the masks as looking like "little black rubber pigs." They were piled in stacks "covering the floor like a growth of black fungus." She sees "a very small child bursting into a wail of dismay on catching sight of its mother disguised in a black snout." In spite of the gas masks, the war doesn't seem real. The months between September, 1939 and May, 1940, become known as the "Phoney War." Urban children, who had been evacuated to the countryside, away from vulnerable cities, are all returned home.

Finally, the illusion ends. On May 10th, 1940, Hitler begins his "drive to the sea." After a mere ten days, on May 20th, Hitler's army occupies France. British and French troops are cut off by the advancing German army. Between May 26th and June 4th, more than 300,000 soldiers are evacuated from the beaches of Northern France. A fleet of British destroyers, other large ships, and the famous "little ships of Dunkirk" return them to England in defeat. A German invasion of Britain now seems inevitable. "Operation Sea Lion," the German plan for a cross Channel invasion, would surely be next. France has fallen with surprising ease. The air defense mounted by the Royal Air Force seems a slim weapon against such a potent enemy. Britain without allies stands alone against the Nazi threat.

All around us uncertainty and fear gain ground. My father has a friend, Alec Bell, whom he describes as a man of "demonic energy." His daughter, sent by her father, suddenly arrives at our house on a bicycle to declare that Paddy and the children must be sent to safety. Alec is organizing a plan to send the children of Oxford University dons (faculty) to the homes of American academic families who are offering sponsorship and foster care. My father describes getting caught up in Alec's "conveyer belt." In an attempt to extricate himself, he protests that he is not a don. Alec tells him not to worry. It is enough that he is a graduate, "an Oxford man." Tom protests that he hasn't any money. Alec assures him that he can pay later. When my father objects that my mother cannot go because she has no passport, Alec tells him again that he needn't worry because his batman in the First World War is now Chief Passport Officer.

The passport arrives overnight. Almost immediately, we are on a train at Euston Station, headed for a port unknown, kept secret because of wartime security. Here are my father's words. "As the tail of the train disappeared up the line I think I must have suddenly realized the enormity of what I had just done. I walked back down the platform doing something I cannot remember having done before or since: weeping absolutely without any inhibition or control, the tears pouring down my face." He didn't see us again for nineteen years.

CHAPTER 2

The Journey

For all of my two and a half years, I have been securely rooted in family and place. Do I remember our journey? When people ask, I say I don't because I do not. But there are the dreams--two dreams which recurred throughout my life, dreams filled with anxiety. In the House Dream, I am in a house that is not mine but is very close to the house that *is* mine, perhaps across the street or in the same neighborhood. I know I am in the wrong house. But I am not merely visiting. I have somehow moved there but I know I must get back to my own house. And I can't. There was a time in my life when I needed, as they say, to "talk to someone." I did, for many years. Overtime, as I talked, the dream changed and then stopped, never to recur. In my final dream, I am in the attic of my house, my own house where I lived with my husband and children for twenty six years. And I am packing suitcases. I am packing. And it is all right.

In the Telephone Dream, I am calling someone important, but I cannot reach them. I cannot make the dial work. As I hold the phone, I have great difficulty speaking. I feel as if I am under water and cannot see and cannot be heard. This is terrible. In my final dream, the "someone" whom I am calling answers the phone. I look out the window and think I see him in the street below. I do remember that when I was somewhere between the ages of five and nine, my mother was on the phone to England, a rare event, and I was near her. There was a globe on the desk next to the phone. I remember the globe. That is all. I don't have this dream anymore.

In the year 2000, my husband and I were invited to visit friends in St. John's, Newfoundland. I said, "Let's drive and stop in Halifax." Halifax, Nova Scotia, where we finally reached safe harbor in August 1940 after nearly two weeks at sea. "Halifax," a name that slips easily from my tongue but as far as my reality is concerned it might have been the moon or the Land of Oz. Halifax is simply part of an old family story. Or so I think until I enter the Pier 21 Museum there a few weeks later, Pier 21, the Ellis Island of Canada, the gateway port to North America during World War II.

I have brought my original landing card with me, a small wrinkled treasure that my mother had saved. It states that I was a passenger on the "Duchess of York" and that the ship arrived August 23, 1940. Maybe I can show my landing card to someone but I don't really know what I am looking for. All I know is that I am here again where our sea journey ended.

I am hungry. I need to eat. I am on a quest and I need strength. My husband and I sit down at a little round table in the museum café. I dive into a bowl of tomato tortellini soup and quench my thirst with a Perrier. As I look up, I see a wide, lighted window above the warehouse-like exhibition space. A nearby sign reads "Resource Center" and we can take the elevator there. A pleasant young man greets us. He is seated at a desk in a room filled with bookcases, books, and several computers.

Fumblingly I explain myself. I show him my landing card. He invites us to sit down and I begin to tell him the story I have told so many times. It has become rote over the years. I could tell it in my sleep. It feels just that disconnected. My story has had a certain cachet at dinner parties. But that is all it is, entertainment over food and wine. I stop talking and say to him, "I don't know how much of this you want to hear." This is where I often end, aware that I may be boring the dinner guests or taking up too much of peoples' time. "Keep going," he says, " I want to hear it. That's what we are here for, to listen to your story."

I am stunned. For the first time in my life I am sitting with a person who is here precisely, specifically, to hear my story. He becomes my quest master, and with the aid of his data bases, oral histories, ships' lists and his own inquisitiveness and listening ear, he is here to guide my journey. There will be no interruptions for a trip to the kitchen for another bottle of wine or after dinner tea or coffee.

I must have come to an ending eventually. Steven, my new fellow search-er, gets up, goes to his files and unearths a photograph and history of the ship, the "Duchess of York." I try to imagine myself on board. For the preceding two years, since the opening of the museum, research staff have been collect-ing narratives from people who entered Canada through Pier 21, including British evacuee children who arrived during WW II. Steven recalls a narra-tive history from a man who, as a child, had traveled on our same ship. He searches his database. He finds the story. The man's name is John. I am no longer alone on my journey.

John was there and he has written about it. My eyes could have seen what he saw. He was 11 years old when he boarded the "Duchess of York" among a group of British children headed for wartime safe keeping in Canada. I read that we sailed on August 10, 1940 in a convoy with other ships carrying a total of 1131 evacuees. There were also three troop carriers. We were escorted by six destroyers and the battleship "HMS Revenge" on our run through these dangerous waters.

The convoy speed was fifteen knots, nearly twice the speed of normal merchant convoys, considered fast enough to outrun enemy submarines. Nonetheless, a ship in our convoy was torpedoed. According to John, we could not turn back for rescue because of our precious cargo, the hundreds of children on board. During our journey John liked to go up on deck and watch the naval escort and the large liner, the "Georgic." The ship was carry-ing German prisoners of war to be interned in North America. He marveled at the lights when we entered Halifax at the end of the journey. My mother had often told me how astonished she was to see so much light after the black-outs of England.

I want to meet this man, John, who has opened the past for me. I want him to know that I was there, too. He returned to England after the war when he was sixteen. Two years later he returned to live in Canada perma-nently. Steven seemed reluctant to give me much information about him, so I did not pursue it.

Nonetheless, I am a grateful explorer. And there are more discoveries to come.

We go back downstairs to tour the museum. The first room we enter had been for disembarking passengers waiting to be processed. I have been here before. My mother has told me what it was like. As we leave the ship she hears people, maybe soldiers guarding the pier, hissing greetings as we pass. It is dark. Here in the museum, the original door entering the receiving area has been left in place. It is painted a dull yellow and over time the wood has become grooved. I walk through it. I touch the frame, the sides, the smoothness of its old surfaces. For the first time, I know deep within me that this really has been my life. It beckons me to my past and now I know that this is my story. It happened to me. I am a fisherwoman. I have hooked the fish. I'm reeling it in, year by year, memory by memory. No longer is it just a dinner party tale in two dimensions, disconnected and distant, served up with coffee and dessert before the guests go home.

A few years ago, when my mother was living near us, in New Hampshire, my husband and I left our Vermont home for a trip to Montreal, a three hour drive. My mother had questioned me about our plans and reminded me that Montreal had been our first destination after leaving our ship in Halifax Harbor in August of 1940. I had not known this. She said we went to Montreal by train.

Maybe it was like this. We ready ourselves to leave the ship. My mother gathers our belongings. How many suitcases have we been allowed to bring? What necessities and small treasures had she managed to pack in those frantic short days before departure? Clothes, of course, but what about the sterling silver napkin rings, engraved with our initials and given to us as infants on our christening day? Mine reads F.A.V. for Felicity Ann Vaughan. I use it every day and as I rub my thumb along the initials, I wonder at its journey. It was my first possession. Had the napkin rings been gifts from a family member or a godparent? Surely, my impecunious parents, struggling to make ends meet, could not buy silver of any kind. Someone in the family must have respected our birth enough to spend a little money on a christening gift. I do not know who that might have been, but I have my napkin ring. It has traveled with me all this way.

Here on the ship there are many children accompanied by volunteer chaperones on their way to host families in Canada. We seem to be the only ones who have a mother. The Bell Canada Ships Database for the "Duchess of York" records a capacity of 580 cabin class, 480 tourist class, and 510 3rd class passengers. We are not a full load, however. The Pier 21 Museum handbook, published in 2000, notes that 3,000 "guest children" passed through its gates during World War II. Between seven and eight hundred children arrived on the "Duchess of York." We might not have been in the count as we were privately sponsored by the Oxford University Evacuation Scheme and not by the Canadian government. We were there nonetheless, scrambling for a place in line among children clutching teddy bears and dolls. This wasn't going off to summer camp nor was it to be a journey of a few months as had been suggested to relinquishing parents in Britain. It was five years before these children were able to go home. My mother, my brother and I never did go "home."

We leave the ship in the dark of night. But I imagine, even at that hour, we are not a bedraggled trio. Photos of us a couple of weeks later in Tennessee show my brother and myself beautifully dressed in matching boy girl outfits. For my mother, clothes were the measure of the woman, almost to the point of vanity. She was beautiful and would exercise her good taste whenever possible, even after two weeks aboard ship crossing dangerous waters.

We must be traveling by train, probably the Ocean Limited of Canadian National Railways, since 1904 serving the Port of Halifax with service to Montreal. Immigrants rode these rails on their way westward to the prairies and this train was critical to travelers during the First and Second World Wars. Hence our journey. We would travel through Nova Scotia and New Brunswick, through towns with brusque English names such as Amherst and Moncton and Rogersville, passing into French Canada with its mellifluous sounds, Petit-Rocher, Trois Pistoles, and Montmagny. The trip would have taken about 24 hours, a journey of 836 miles. In a recently discovered letter, I find that my mother had received an offer of help. My speculations take substance:

18th August
Dear Mrs. Vaughan —

I have exchanged letters with Miss Burleson concerning the arrival of you and your two children. It would be my pleasure if I may be of assistance to you in any way.

My fiancée, Miss Pamela Milligan, and six children destined for homes in New Mexico, crossed on the boat with you. We plan to proceed to Montreal; that is a rail-head for points in the United States, and I am hoping that you will feel free to join us. If the suggestion meets with your approval, and if Miss Burleson has not succeeded in making arrangements to meet you, I can secure accommodations for all of us at the Hotel Windsor in Montreal and we can plan our routes from that point.

In case you are short of funds I would be happy to save you any embarrassment while you are communicating with Miss Burleson (Roan Hill, Johnson City, Tennessee) who tells me that she will send funds to meet the expenses of the journey south upon hearing from you.

Trusting that your voyage was interesting and not too hard. Welcome to this shore, and looking forward to meeting you in the morning. Greetings.

Deric Nusbaum

I will be wearing a brown tweed coat and dark grey flannels — and am fairly tall.

Christine Burleson, our sponsor, enters our lives, ready with connections and funds to ease our way to our new home in Tennessee. Deric, in his brown and grey clothes, is her messenger. He has a single moment walk-on in this drama, as do his fiancée and the six children bound for New Mexico. But in his letter he brings me news.

I believe our stay in Montreal was only overnight to change trains. My mother had remembered the name of our hotel. My husband and I located it during our visit that year, but I now struggle to find its name anywhere among my scribblings. Why isn't she here to remind me? I am a writer-down-of things in journals, on bits of paper and in calendars. I pore through boxes stuffed with miscellany in my office, among them manila envelopes labeled "Halifax." I consult the Internet and Google "Montreal Hotels 1940." Is it the Berkeley? The name sounds right, touches a memory nerve, but the photos on the archived postcard look nothing like the hotel we stood in front of when we traveled up from Vermont. I am helpless as I try to reconstruct this bit of the past, this particular link in a chain of memories. I blame myself for giving it undue importance. I think of maps for treasure hunters. X marks the spot. As I pick my way through boxes and bags of my mother's saved letters and photos, my searching fingers find Deric Nusbaum's letter. Another blank filled in. I learn that we did take the train and that we stayed at the Windsor Hotel.

As we depart Montreal for New York (our next stop) an unseen hand guides our southward journey. We have a sponsor, required for anyone entering the United States as an evacuee or refugee during the war years. We are on our way to Tennessee and to the home of Christine Burleson, a single woman in her forties who had done graduate work at Oxford. She now lives with her father, Dean of the State Teacher's College in Johnson City. She wants to "do something for the war effort" and has agreed to sponsor us, a mother and two children. A doctor friend of hers meets us in New York, and settles us into a hotel. He also takes care of Peter, who has a cold. My mother remembers how nice he was and said he took us to the Central Park Zoo. The summer is very hot and Paddy decides to cool herself by putting her head out the window for a breath of air. But she is stopped abruptly by her first encounter with a window screen. It is a shock, as there are no such obstructions in English windows. Other than this frequently told story, I know nothing else about the rest of our journey.

Once we arrive in Johnson City, however, we are on record--front page news in the local press. As I write now, I stop to remove yellowed newsprint from its plastic protective envelope. I marvel at its survival. I have faulted my mother at times for her efficiency in downsizing the past by means of tag sales. I have challenged her over the years as to the whereabouts of certain childhood treasures, such as the green cuckoo clock that hung on my bedroom wall in our Minnesota home. I had treasured it so. She denied all knowledge of it. Mostly likely, she had sold it in the neighborhood. And it wasn't just the small things. Once my brother and I were away at college, she thought we didn't need our four bedroom house and sold it. It had been in a friendly neighborhood, but she and my stepfather moved to a dark depressing apartment on the wrong side of Grand Avenue in St. Paul. When I came home from college for holidays, I had to sleep on a day bed in the dining room. When I mentioned this over the years, she seemed unaware that the lack of privacy could have been a problem for me. I certainly never understood why my brother had been allotted one of the three bedrooms.

However, photographs and letters she kept close and forever. For this I am profoundly grateful. For here we are, immediately upon our arrival in Tennessee, in the newspaper and in pictures, "Safe from Hitler's Raiding Planes" in bold face opposite a large photo of my mother and myself, a chubby two year old. She is standing, with me in front of her. We are facing the camera and her arms are extended downward as she grasps my little upraised hands in hers, our fingers entwined. She wears a full length housecoat, with short puffy sleeves, which zips up the front. It is decorated with a sailboat motif, a curious choice considering our recent dangerous ten days at sea. Her hair is hidden, tied up in a small scarf, as if she hadn't had time to wash it. I am wearing a sunsuit and a little bonnet with a sunshade brim. She wears a half smile on her lips and my mouth is a bit open, as if I am about to say something. There is an accompanying photo of my brother and myself on a bed. I sit up looking straight into the camera, happily anticipating the next adventure, while Peter is sound asleep, a hot little boy described as "her exhausted twin brother who simply couldn't stay awake, even to have his picture made.!"

The headline shouts "English Woman Here Has No Doubt Britain Will Win."

Overnight, Paddy has become the voice of Britain in East Tennessee. "There is simply no doubt we will win the war!" declares "this attractive young British matron arriving in Johnson City this week to spend the 'duration' with Miss Christine Burleson at the Burleson home on Roan Hill."

Winston Churchill would have been proud of her. "We shall fight on the beaches, we shall fight on the seas…we shall never surrender." Paddy has taken the fight to these American hills. Both she and Winston turn out to be right but five more years have yet to pass, years that began in near defeat at Dunkirk and eventually involve the entire world. It becomes no longer simply a British war.

CHAPTER 3
What We Left Behind

I TAKE A DEEP BREATH. Here we are in Tennessee, exhausted but presumably safe. But what of those we left behind? Father, grandparents, aunts, uncles, friends, our home in Lyndworth Close, our town of Oxford with it's "dreaming spires." What about the other life we might have led had we not rushed forth, or been pushed, precipitously, into a future not of our choosing? Our frantic travels have ended for now. But we have been ripped from our families, our history, perhaps forever. What have we lost? Who are we?

Our family lived in Oxford where both my parents had deep roots. My mother was born in 1914, the youngest of seven children. The six before her were boys. My grandmother must have been delighted with her pretty baby girl. My mother was always pretty, even at 92. She was named Lilian, after her mother, but took on a nickname in her teens and was known as Paddy for the rest of her life.

Paddy's parents, my maternal grandparents, were working class, fixed firmly in place by the British class system. My grandmother worked as a seamstress, my grandfather was a grocer's assistant. Paddy was always deliberately vague about her family background. Her father drank too much and physically abused her mother, so much so that Paddy feared for her mother's safety. Her father wasn't always that way, she told me. He changed after the suicide of their son, Bill. Just before his wedding in 1933, Bill put his head in the gas oven and died. Bill, the musician, who had his own band and who had lied about his age so that he could fight in the First World War. He was captured and spent time in a German prison camp. He came home but the nightmares pursued him. The doctor told my grandmother that he was as much a casualty of the war as if he had actually died in it. My mother discovered his body when she came home from work. She was alone until others arrived. She was then instructed to make the tea, the British solution to every crisis, meant to stiffen the upper lip.

My grandmother, Lilian Dubber (nee Earl) was born upstairs in a pub in Oxford in 1878, the oldest of sixteen children. I learned the place of her birth only recently as my husband and I walked along St. Giles with a cousin, Richard Dubber. "Our grandmother was born there," he said, pointing to a round blue sign with a golden eagle in flight carrying a baby in its claws. The Eagle and Child still thrives after more than three centuries and is well known as the gathering place in the 1930's and 1940's of a writers' group. The Inklings included C.S. Lewis and J.R.R. Tolkien. We went in for a glass of wine where the barmaid was selling Eagle and Child tee shirts. I tried to tell her my story but she wasn't interested. For me, however, it is a bright piece, retrieved from the broken mirror of my war disrupted past.

Here I have two photographs of the very large Earl family taken when the children were young adults. In one photograph, my great grandmother Liza, a small dumpy woman in black, sits surrounded by her seven daughters who are standing, all smartly dressed, hair well coiffed. My grandmother, Lilian, sits furthest to her mother's left. She is already married and has children of her own. She is wearing a wedding ring of twenty-four carat gold that I wear on the fourth finger of my right hand. The other daughters are my great aunts. I never knew them.

In the partner photograph, my great grandfather, Henry Earl, sits surrounded by his eight sons, all grown to handsome men. They are outside in front of a stone building, which is blurry in the background. Three of the young men stand in the back row and three are seated alongside their father. Two sit crosslegged on small oriental carpets placed on the ground. They are arranged in front of a small leafless tree. Is it spring or autumn? Each one wears a three-piece suit, perhaps custom made by their father, for he was a gentleman's tailor and made suits for Oxford University undergraduates. My great grandfather and four of his sons wear the ribbon of the Royal Order of Foresters draped around their necks. They are exceptionally good-looking, beautifully groomed for the occasion, hair perfectly in place, mustaches precisely trimmed. They are my great uncles whom I also never knew. I am astonished to think of the size of this family and all those who came after. I spent my growing up years with only my mother and brother as family. We were evacuees, strangers in our strange American land where at least we spoke the same language as the natives.

My mother's paternal side, the Dubbers, are solid Anglo Saxon stock, blue eyed and fair skinned, who had surely lived in England since its beginnings. I always imagined they had dubbed knights, earls, and lords, ceremoniously in castles and great houses. But I am wrong here. I have since learned that Dubber is a very rare English surname, originating in medieval times. It derives from the French word "dubbere" or "douber," meaning one who works with gold. Doubers were bookbinders and illustrators, skilled in the use of gold leaf and paint in the preparation of books. It was a guild name and hence one of great status.

My father's family, in some of its elements, was very different and rather foreign. Thomas Hugh Vaughan, my father, was born in Calcutta, India, in 1911. His father, my grandfather, Hugh Christopher Vaughan, was a young engineer from Oxford who went out to India in 1903. His job was to help in building the Victoria Memorial in Calcutta, an architectural tribute to Queen Victoria, Empress of India. He became ill with typhoid, was hospitalized, and there met a young Anglo Indian nurse, Ruth Gertrude Murray, whom he married on the 18th of December 1909 at the Office of the Senior Marriage Registrar of Calcutta. So it says here on their marriage certificate, a large yellowed document held together by cracked tape, miraculously intact after a hundred years. My great aunt, Stella Murray, Ruth Gertrude's sister, witnessed the ceremony, as did James Henry Jennaway, unknown to me. The court fee was ½ Rupee. I found this certificate while sorting out treasures in my father's tiny apartment in Surrey, England, after his death in 1994. There is also my father's Baptismal Certificate. "Thomas Hugh, son of Hugh Christopher and Ruth Gertrude Vaughan, baptized 1911, June 18, said to be born, 1911, May 8th. Baptism solemnized at St. Thomas' Church (Free School), Calcutta."

There is some debate in family circles as to the ethnicity of Ruth Gertrude. Was she Anglo-Indian? The term can have two meanings. There are the Anglo-Indians in the colonial sense. They were English people who lived out their lives in India and may even have been born there, doing the "work of Empire." My great grandfather, on my father's side, Hubert Murray, went out to India probably from Scotland in the late nineteenth century to work for the Eastern Telegraph Company. He married at least twice. My grandmother, Ruth Gertrude, was one of six children of his first marriage.

Anglo-Indian also denotes those of mixed European and Indian parentage. This may be a more accurate description of my grandmother. Ruth Gertrude met her husband's family when she arrived in England with him in 1914, their three year old son, Tom, in tow. When she was introduced at a family gathering, a shocked brother in law is reported to have exclaimed within the hearing of all present "My God, she's black!" She never spoke to him again. However, paternity determined nationality in those days, and Ruth, whatever her hue, surely believed herself to be English, like her father. Strangely, she never allowed her oldest son, my father, to forget that he didn't belong in England at all, nor did she. She was never happy there.

In 2007, during a trip to India and the city of Calcutta, now known as Kolkata, I had the opportunity to explore this titillating bit of family history. I had been wondering what it meant to be Anglo-Indian, a person of mixed blood, Indian and European. I learned that these Anglo Indians began to leave India in 1947 at the end of British colonial rule. Many emigrated to Australia and New Zealand. There was no place for them in an independent India. They had always seen themselves as English but they weren't, nor did they want to be Indian.

While in Kolkata, I met an Anglo Indian woman, Maureen. I asked her many questions. She was light olive skinned, beautiful at eighty four, stylishly dressed in a black pant suit trimmed with gold braid. Anglo Indians, she said, always wore European dress. I remembered that, in 1967, I had appeared dressed in a sari at my father's London home after my return from three years in New Delhi where my husband and I had lived during a Foreign Service posting. My Auntie Stella, my grandmother's sister, who had come "home" to England in 1947, was there with us. (Of course it could not have been "home" since she had never been there before.) I do not think she was pleased to see me thus dressed. At the time I could not have understood why. I thought she would like the touch of India that I brought with me.

Maureen explained that the English had used Anglo Indians to do less prestigious (but quite necessary) jobs, exploited them, fostered their illusion that they were somehow "English," and then left them after Independence to fend for themselves. European men often left behind Indian and Anglo Indian women they had married, as well as the children they had fathered, as had Maureen's own British husband. Over tea we talked about my grandfather's choice. Did he have any idea that his wife might not be thoroughly English? Nor his son? Would it have mattered to him? Was he particularly courageous in returning to England with her. Or simply naïve?

Here is Ruth Gertrude in a photo, a young woman wearing a floor length white dress with a high collar and long sleeves. The dress is nipped in at the waist and full in the bosom. She wears a brooch at her throat. She is photographed with four other young women, similarly dressed. It is a class photo, a nursing class. Her complexion is darker than those of three others, but not as dark as the one standing behind her. Here she is again, decades later in England, at the wedding of her younger son, Peter. Wrap her in a sari and she becomes a rather plain looking middle-aged Indian woman. Here is my father, in the same photo, a tall, black haired young man. When I arrived in India in 1964, I was astonished to see his likeness in tall Sikh men with their high cheekbones and narrow faces. Put a turban on my father and he becomes a Sardar, a Sikh.

But I must resist the temptation to carry on with the Indian story, though there is much to tell. For now I will simply say that Hugh Christopher, Ruth Gertrude, and their little son, Thomas, three years old, left India for England in 1914 at the outbreak of WWI. Though technically British-born by virtue of India being part of the British Empire, Ruth had never been "home" to England.

During the sea passage, there was an accident to their ship. Ruth Gertrude believed they had been chased by enemy submarines. My father remembers being carried through a flooded passageway. As they left the cabin, he saw his mattress floating in the water. Twenty three years later, he sent his own children off into the dangerous waters of another war.

My father's family on the paternal side were more traditionally rooted. My great grandfather, Thomas Browne Vaughan, was a Welsh clergyman who fathered six children. Here they are, two boys and two girls sitting in a cart. Another girl sits astride the donkey that is pulling the cart. There is a third boy dressed in black who looks like a vicar in miniature. He faces us, so that we will know that he is the oldest and to be taken more seriously than these other children. There is a young man holding the bridle of the sleepy donkey. The little girl sitting on the donkey is pretty. Her long hair falls in soft curls over her left shoulder.

The children range in age from five to 12; a guess, but they are certainly close together. My grandfather, Hugh Christopher, is the youngest. The girls are Mildred, Gwenydd, and Gwladys. None married. As adults they lived with their widowed mother in the cathedral town of Lincoln. One ran orphan homes, another was a teacher, and the third gave her time at a free dental clinic. Gwenydd lost a leg in France on Armistice Day in 1918 when she was nurse at a base hospital. She had been run over by a truck.

The aunts and their mother, my great grandmother, Agnes Coleman Vaughan, took Ruth Gertrude and young Thomas into their home during WWI. Hugh Christopher was away at war for nearly five years. My father adored his aunts. Throughout his life they were a source of support to him. His own mother seems to have been difficult and critical. She was unhappy in what was supposedly her native country. She harbored resentments which remained throughout her life. I have an image of her in my mind but it is nothing but scraps. She was my grandmother who looked upon me, surely must have held me in her arms, touched me. I existed for her, probably even in my absence. But to me she is only a story. My mother told of her hot curries that made you perspire. But you didn't want to stop eating. That is about all I knew,

My father's autobiography, written when he was in his late 70's, yields this history for me. Ruth Gertrude considered my mother's pregnancy a disgrace to the family, as was my mother with her working class background. On the other hand, the aunts were quite willing to approve the marriage. They even took us into their home once when my parents wanted a short vacation. Paddy and Tom were staying at a pub in Shropshire owned by the parents of a friend, near a large Royal Air Force base. In his autobiography, from which I have gleaned a bit of history, my father describes how officers and "other ranks" came for drinks and camaraderie. Overhearing their conversations, he suddenly realized that war was imminent. My parents quickly ended their holiday and collected us from the aunts in Lincoln. We returned to Oxford. Two weeks later, on September 3, 1939, Britain, along with France, Australia, and New Zealand, declared war on Germany in response to the Nazi invasion of Poland. Peter and I were not quite two years old.

By now we have become very much a part of the picture, and, in my father's words, we are very beautiful. Friends of Paddy and Tom visit often, intrigued by the babies who have made their parents into instant celebrities. Peter is a small, wiry, active boy engrossed in figuring out how things work, off on his own little missions. I am large and plump and contented. My people skills are already well honed. According to my father, I would pick out my prey "with instant stereoscopy and before you knew where you were would be ensconced on the most eligible male knee."

We live a few houses down from our Granny Vaughan in the Headington neighborhood of Oxford. We have many relatives arrayed around us. Our Grandma and Grandfather Dubber live in Cowley, an adjoining part of town, home to the large factories of Pressed Steel and Morris Motors. We go to Granny Dubber's for the Sunday roast and Yorkshire pudding. Food is family history and this recipe has been passed down through my mother to my brother and me. Beat the batter until large bubbles froth. Let it stand for at least hour. Beat it again. The fat in the pan must be spitting hot before you pour in the batter. Do not open the oven door as it cooks. Wait out the required cooking time. Then hold your breath and cross your fingers. Open oven door. Be gratified. It has "yorked," my word for rising without benefit of baking powder but simply from the combination of well beaten eggs, milk, and flour. Consume while hot and steamy and crispy. With roast beef, of course.

My mother takes us out in the double pram. I am at the far end because I am heavier than Peter. We wear boy and girl versions of matching outfits, hand knit by Granny Dubber. One day at home there is a frightening event. We are in our cribs, which we have learned to rock across the floor. One of us rocks into the wall heater and the mattress catches on fire. Our screams alert our mother and friends downstairs who rush to our rescue. The friend heaves the mattress, minus us, out the window. "One of us" is how I remember other dramatic and threatening events in our early years. Who hit the wall heater? Who pushed whom into the fishpond in Tennessee? Who pulled the other one out of the surf in Florida? Twins with a merged memory function. We have each claimed the heroic role even though one of us had to have been the pusher and the pulled. The truth eludes us still.

CHAPTER 4

Life On Roan Hill

THOSE WE LOVED AND WHO loved us vanish, not gradually but abruptly, suddenly excised from our lives. The war is far away. Now we begin our American life with a Southern flavor. We are living with Christine and her father. She likes us. I have unearthed a letter recently that she wrote on September 1, 1940, soon after our arrival:

> *"Dear Miss Everett,*
>
> *Your selection is proving most delightfully right. Never have I enjoyed any guests more than the Vaughans. Peter and Felicity are a source of constant joy; their mother is very congenial and easy to live with, fitting in smoothly to our atmosphere. My only trouble is resisting the temptation to play with them hour after hour. They are at an enchanting age and of really superior quality. Peter is quick and of a mechanical turn, Felicity is demure and babyish. Last week we had a tea party with other twins about five months older but I thought ours outshined them quite. Mrs. Vaughan is a good mother, in control of them, sweet and cheerful but firm...Do please tell Mr. Kenneth Bell how delighted I am with the selection. He rushed them over here just in time, it seems to us."*

Christine's house is large and white and brick. That much is certain as I have a photo to prove it. The Gone With The Wind style faux Grecian pillars of my imaginings also must have been there. I remember a *porte cochere* where cars could draw up to the entrance of the house, protected from inclement weather. Once I was found there lying in the back seat of a car, unhappy and unwilling to come inside. Are our earliest memories the sad and difficult ones? Perhaps our miseries touch us first because they require something more than do our happy moments. I know I was very miserable then.

The Burleson home is an estate. We are settled into the little gatehouse. There are household servants, one in particular I remember was a "Negro" boy named Rudolph. Here we are with him in a small, scalloped-edged black and white photo riding in a pony cart. Rudolph holds the reins. Peter and I sit next to him, the two of us squashed tightly together. I take a magnifying glass for a closer look. I'm between Peter and Rudolph. We are holding something, perhaps a stuffed animal for comfort. The horse is any horse. The white brick house is behind us.

I have a few other photos. They are larger and the magnifying glass almost does the job of bringing life to the black and white. We are in the garden, an expanse of lawn surrounded by well-tended flower beds and wooded borders. In one photo, Peter is downstage left, very solemn faced, pointing directly at the photographer with his right hand, his left hand in the pocket of his overalls. My mother and I are center stage slightly to the right. She is bending over me, intent on fixing a barrette into my short hair. She is slim and wears a knee-length short sleeved floral printed dress. I have placed my left hand, palm outward, over my mouth. Is it to keep from speaking or perhaps from crying? She always pulled my hair rather fiercely when she fixed it, or later, when she braided it. Peter and I are identically dressed in overalls which have a small embroidered design on the front panel. We wear striped long sleeved tee shirts underneath. A stuffed panda and another soft toy animal lie abandoned on the ground. In the next photo we are on the ground, crouched next to a large black and white rabbit, which is very much alive. We are delighted and I reach out to touch it with a tentative finger. Here is Christine in another photo, on her hands and knees in the grass while Peter and I stand nearby looking down. All of us are engrossed in something on the ground, perhaps the rabbit. She is a slim attractive young woman with dark hair and properly dressed in skirt and blouse.

Here is the most wonderful photo of all. The two of us are perched in a stone bird- bath (no water, no birds, just us), surely posed for posterity or the local rag. I think we are a little older as my hair has grown a bit. And again we are wearing matching twin fashion statements, little white short sleeved shirts underneath a jumper with skirt for me and short pants with a bib top for Peter. There is no question but that we are quite adorable and dark haired unlike our blonde mother. Again I am looking directly into the camera as usual. Peter is looking into the beyond, eyes drawn to another interest.

"Christine", only by this name have I known her. Recently, however, my curiosity has brought her more clearly into focus. Aided by search technology, I discovered that Christine Burleson, the daughter of the Dean, was a widely respected Shakespeare scholar, and gifted teacher at the college for more than forty years. I have also learned that she is the main character in her own tragic story, which culminates in her death by suicide in 1967. Entering students at the college today are still told that her ghost haunts the school building named after her father.

But let us not go there now for it would be a distraction from our current tale. Let us keep her here in the days when she took us in and provided us with a home in times of terrible disruption. Hers was an act of courage and innocent good intent.

CHAPTER 5

Time Out For Travel of a Different Kind

IT IS DECEMBER, 1940. CHRISTINE takes us on a road trip to see America—or at least her part of it. We make a 2,600 mile journey from Johnson City to Charleston, Savannah, Jacksonville, Daytona Beach, Vero Beach, Palm Beach, Miami, Sarasota, and Atlanta, before returning to East Tennessee. Here is a typed, single-spaced four page letter that Paddy wrote to her mother in England, entitled "An Outline of our Floridian Trip," saved in carbon copy, crumply now but otherwise quite intact and easy to read.

It is an astonishing piece of writing, filled with vivid detail. She intersperses the letter with her commentary and observations about people she met and places she saw. She must have taken notes or kept a daily trip journal. She could not possibly have recreated all this from memory. She was a scribbler down of things, like me. In her later years, she made neat little daily jottings in her UNICEF calendar, noting the small events of a rather ordinary life, such as whom she saw that day and what she cooked for dinner. Perhaps she went for a swim in the condominium pool or had lunch with a friend on Nicollet Mall. Her Florida journal is so much more than this. It's an extraordinary gift from a turbulent past.

She begins. "We left Johnson City on a chilly December morning about 8.30 a.m. – all well wrapped up and the heater on inside the car. We were a party of five – Christine, Mrs. Divine, Peter, Felicity, and myself."

Who is Mrs. Divine? A servant, a friend? There is no explanation. Our first stop is Charleston. "It was in this town that I noticed the coloured folk seem much darker than those back in Tennessee and far greater in number. Also there were lots of gay young cadets floating around in grey and navy blue tightly-fitting uniforms which showed up their waistlines and looked quite smart so long as the wearer had kept his figure! Before leaving here we took the twins to some gardens in which were kept some lovely birds and a few animals, such as deer, bears and monkeys – and we all enjoyed ourselves immensely feeding them with nuts and popcorn."

We go the Magnolia Gardens near Charleston. "We turned off the main highway into a lonely road with trees on one side and a somber swamp on the other, out of which rose ghostly trees heavily laden with grey moss. So thick was the growth that it must have strangled the life out of the trees and the trunks and branches were void of leaves and were deathly white like skeletons bleached in the sun…as if an army of ghosts had risen from the swamp with their arms weakly held out all dripping with grey slimy mud."

We pass on down to Florida; and, after a good breakfast in St. Augustine, Paddy writes, "We went in search of the 'Fountain of Youth', which we found and then drank the waters thereof – and so, even if the war goes on for ten years you will find us all looking exactly the same when we meet again." Handsome cadets in uniforms, ghostly armies, a long war, images of her imagination now but all too real in the world she has so recently left. She is not so far away from it after all.

At Vero Beach, we stop and "let the children wade in the warm sea and make their first sand castles…Felicity was very brave and loved to feel her tiny feet in the water, but Peter didn't care much for it and preferred to dig in the sand – naturally the adults got a tremendous thrill by holding their own skirts high and frisking in the waves."

I try to imagine my grandma in her little house in Cowley, Oxford, England, (the full mailing address was always thus), reading this cheerful message.

How much did she miss us? Perhaps her sadness was tinged with a little guilty sense of relief that we were out of sight, out of mind, the daughter who had brought some measure of shame on the family with her hasty wedding and quickly born children. Years later, when I knew my grandma, she made an oblique reference to something she could tell me, but wouldn't. She appeared to want me know but it was as if the words could never pass her lips.

Our third birthday arrives on December 12th and we celebrate it in Madeira Beach, a town lying between the Gulf of Mexico and St. Petersburg. We are staying in a bungalow on the beach, where a pathway from the back door goes down to the sea. Christine and Mrs. Devine have left us there for what turns out to be three happy days. Why they have done so is not clear, but it doesn't matter. "Everyone was so kind, and some people took us out fishing for the day (on the twins' birthday.) And I must say I doubt very much if most people in that town had ever seen twins before – the way everyone noticed ours was simply amazing – it was even worse than usual and the poor man who was with us must have felt very conspicuous, though actually I think he enjoyed it."

"Our" twins? Who is the "our?" A slip of the tongue to include our absent father, or merely a reference to Christine and Mrs. Devine? We continue our journey through Sarasota where we visit the winter headquarters of The Ringling Brothers Circus. Here we are in two photos! In one Peter and I are seated on a low wall in front of an open tent where large tusked heads are dimly visible in the background. My mother is standing behind us, her head lowered as she appears to be looking either at the ground or at us, her hands open at her sides. It is not a happy stance. I am reminded of her lifelong intense dislike of zoos. Caged animals always evoked horror in her.

Next to her is a smiling woman, a respectable-looking matron in a dark suit and hat. This must be Mrs. Devine, hardly the household retainer of my imagination. Christine must be behind the camera. Peter and I each clutch a stuffed toy, mine is a monkey, and again we are dressed alike, boy girl versions, little white shoes and socks on our feet. Peter's clothes seem more to be a boy version of mine than mine are a girl version of his, if this makes sense. It is evident by now that I am growing to be a little bit bigger than he is. Paddy wears a short-sleeved belted striped dress that would not look out of place today. In the second photo, Peter and I are seated by ourselves and the elephants are more in evidence behind us.

We travel on to Tarpon Springs and the sponge market and Greek divers who ask my mother if she is English when they hear her speak. "I suppose they felt quite matey," she writes. What was this about, I wonder. A small international flirtation among the sponges between representatives of two currently war-beleaguered nations? Good looking Greek meets attractive British girl? Down with the Italians and the Germans? The stuff of movies and my imagination only.

Next we see the glass bottomed boats at Dade City, then Atlanta and reminiscences of Gone With the Wind and finally home in Tennessee. "It was the grandest trip I have ever had and Christine certainly saw to it that we did plenty of sight-seeing. If I really went into detail about everything it would fill a book, so I hope you can gather a fairly good impression from this brief outline."

CHAPTER 6

Moving On

WE ARE SETTLED DOWN AT Roan Hill for "the duration." But what of that distant war we are enduring? It is December, 1940. German air raids are targeting major British cities. It is the "Blitz." German bombs damage St. Paul's Cathedral in London. Meanwhile, Hitler is secretly planning his attack on the Soviet Union to begin a few months hence in June of 1941. The United States is not yet in the war and American public opinion still regards it as a European conflict best avoided.

It is Christmas in Tennessee, our first American Christmas, and we have been three years old for two entire weeks and in our new home for four months. We certainly look happy facing the camera again. I am lying on my tummy, Peter is half kneeling. We have planted ourselves under a tree loaded with ornaments and tinsel, open presents arrayed around us. We push up, heads raised, smiles bright for someone in the room who is out of sight. As usual, I look straight at the camera, really laughing. Peter is smiling but a little more subdued. Here I am, the center stage child throughout my life. Peter is more removed, more the observer. He eventually becomes a successful theater critic in his professional life. How early are we formed. A great deal of time passes before life allows us the luxury of looking back. Then we can be astonished as we glimpse how we have become who we are.

The months of our stay go by and become a year and the year stretches into another. Neither Paddy nor Christine could possibly have anticipated that what began as a brief rescue mission would become a living arrangement with no known end. Inevitably tension develops between the two of them.

I have only Paddy's side of the story. She talked about Christine a few years ago while responding to a question from her grandson, Thom, Peter's son. I was there as well.

"She was a nice person" she said, "and she liked you children a lot. I think she was jealous. If I were invited somewhere, she wanted to be invited too. She should be, she said, as I was her guest. She liked to sew. She made that blue velvet housecoat for me. Her friends, the Baldwins, were wonderful. There was a violin concert. Albert Spaulding invited me and Christine came, too. But there was a party afterwards and I couldn't go. She wouldn't let me go." I have a photo of Paddy in the blue velvet floor length housecoat. I remember it well. It fit her perfectly and she wore for it for many years.

My mother has often described the restrictions that Christine put on her life. She was not allowed to go about on her own except to town in the afternoon to pick up the mail or to visit the Baldwins across the way. They were an English couple who took a great interest in us and were very kind. Eventually, they were instrumental in helping Paddy make her departure from Roan Hill. My father mentions in his autobiography that he received a letter from Christine filled with an angry account of Paddy's egregious behavior. Details are missing and must be left to our imagination. Perhaps an affair, something of a sexual nature, which would not have been out of character.

The actual event which precipitated our leaving was quite innocuous. Christine complained that the tin cans we used for play in the bath were scratching the tub. This was the end for Paddy. She picked us out of the bath, got us dressed, packed up our few things, and immediately went across the road to the Baldwins to seek help. She had no money and no way of getting any. By now, the Japanese had blown up American ships at Pearl Harbor. America is at war. We are leaving Roan Hill but where can we go?

CHAPTER 7
Life On A Florida Beach

THE OIL IS EVERYWHERE. COVERING the beach, floating on the surface of the sea. The war has arrived at the doorstep of our little house on Atlantic Beach near Jacksonville. I only remember that we are kept from our sandy playground that day. Since then I have learned that, at night, a German U-Boat had sunk an oil-filled American tanker just off shore. Now as I write, I want to know more. I am the fisherwoman, this time tossing out my Google line as bait. The cyber ocean yields a catch. I find an ABC News Florida affiliate FCN report dated April 9, 2012. It blares forth the news. "German Sub Sinks a U.S. Tanker, 70 Years Ago." I learn that the "SS Gulfamerica" went down just off Ponte Vedra Beach near Jacksonville on April 10, 1942. I am astonished. We were there.

According to reports, local residents had flocked to the beach when they saw flames, glaring orange and red, and black smoke. It had occurred at night before the imposition of blackout. The oil tanker was outlined against the lights of the Jacksonville Beach fairgrounds, clearly visible to the German submarine. Many years later it was learned that the U-Boat commander had maneuvered his ship between the coast and the tanker to enable him to fire out to sea, perhaps to avoid hitting the civilians on the beach. But who was to know at the time? It is a bizarre scene: people in cars on the beach watching the tanker burn.

The Baldwins, generous and caring friends, neighbors of Christine, had given us the $75 that got us here. Their son, Lynn, is in the Navy stationed at the recently commissioned Naval Air Station. He is our contact, but what could he possibly do for us? Paddy may have known him in Tennessee or she may have never seen him before. Maybe he was involved in the egregious incident that sparked Christine's enraged letter to my father. But I don't know. Paddy herself always said that she went to Florida in the hopes of finding a job, as money from my father was now almost impossible to get.

How we loved that beach! We had such joy there. When my father, a widower going blind, died alone in his sleep in his tiny apartment in Long Ditton, Surrey, in 1994, Peter and I went together to sort through his possessions. There we found a great treasure: a little box containing a roll of 8 mm color film, labeled "Peter and Felicity, Jacksonville, Florida, 1942." Paddy, Peter, and Felicity in color that is still bright, though a bit fuzzy, on a day at the beach. There we are running back and forth, in and out of the waves, rolling up the legs of our red overalls, getting stripped down by our mother. She inserts us into our bathing suits and sends us off to the water with a little push. She wears a one-piece shiny blue swim suit. She is as beautiful as ever with her blonde hair shoulder-length and loose, with a neat center part. She seems delighted with her children. We are indeed delightful. Here I am, eyes closed, looking up and smiling, as I catch the warmth of the sun on my face. The surf is modest but just enough to excite us. She encourages us to look at the camera as the three of us move in the ankle-deep water facing the anonymous photographer.

The scene changes. Now we are walking out of our house, down the driveway toward the unknown filmmaker. I am ready for the camera and happy to show off my baby buggy and dolls as I stride confidently forward. Peter is not so happy. He flaps his hands in frustration as he turns his back and drops from view. My mother comes out of our small white cottage. She has changed into a dress, green with a white floral pattern. The skirt falls just below the knee and moves gently around her legs as it is caught by the breeze. She carries a lighted cigarette in her right hand, more an affectation of sophistication than the food of an addiction. "I don't inhale," she always claimed until she gave it up in her 70's.

The camera moves in for a closeup. Her lips are full and very red with lipstick. She looks young and vulnerable. She is still only twenty eight years old. Is it my imagination, or does she resemble a young Queen Elizabeth? There is that particularly English look which is hard to describe, but I know it when I see it. She kneels and gathers us to her, Peter on her right and me on her left. We look quite happy and are smiling for the camera. The white circles flash, signaling the end of the reel. Somehow this film reached my father in London and it was in his keeping until he died. Did he wonder who was behind the camera, a lover, perhaps? He was always ready to condemn her for what he viewed as her promiscuity. What did he think of the film, seeing us like that? Did he long for us, mourn us, had he somehow managed conveniently to rationalize our absence as "the best thing for the children?"

My very first memories, those that I can claim as my own as opposed to the remembered stories told by my mother, emerge from our days in that little house on the beach. By now we are four and a half years old. Peter and I plant peach pits in the driveway hoping that trees will grow there. I remember our terrible sunburns and my mother peeling off my dress, a stiff scratchy organdy thing that hurt with every tug. Paddy knew nothing of the Florida sun and how it could singe our delicate little English skins.

On another occasion, Paddy was looking for a set of keys which she could not find. We led her down to the beach and showed her where they were hidden between the stones in a low sea-wall, either forgotten by her or put there through some mischief of ours. Many years ago, on a business trip to Jacksonville, I went to Atlantic Beach carrying the address of the little white cottage in which we had lived. It had somehow made its way onto the back of Paddy's first Social Security card. I looked for the wall but found only something very low and very small. But we were very low and very small in those days too. There were no peach trees or even a familiar looking house. But the street, 7th street, does go right down to the beach and the sea beyond. I remember a visit to the mess at the Naval Air Station where we stood in line with our sectioned metal trays to get our food. We probably were the guests of the mysterious Lynn who appears here and there in photographs. He is handsome and black-haired in a sailor's uniform.

CHAPTER 8

A Minnesota Winter

WE CAN'T STAY. PADDY NEEDS a job and gets an unusual offer. Lynn has a friend, stationed with him in Jacksonville, whose parents live on a farm in Minnesota. They say they will take us in if my mother will help with the chores. She accepts and off we go. Even though I can remember bits of our Florida days, I have no memory of the journey to Minnesota. Did these good people send us money for the train ride? What do they know about us? Their son is in the Navy and perhaps in harm's way. Perhaps they think this good deed will insulate them, magically, from the bad things, the unthinkable loss of their son in combat. Or, maybe like Christine, they want to "do something for the war effort" and are looking for a way to reach beyond their comfortable civilian life in the rural heartland.

We are there for winter, 1942 into 1943. They are Margaret and Tom. For a few months we, a family of strangers, make a life together. Tom runs the dairy farm and Margaret teaches in the one room schoolhouse. Paddy bakes bread and chops wood, strong even though she weighs no more than 100 pounds on a heavy day. She gains strength for the chopping by imagining that the logs are "Japs." She is still fighting her personal war, now from a Minnesota farm.

Here we are in four photographs, smiling. Peter and I are standing on snow- covered ground. Behind us is what looks like a grape arbor and behind that the barn. In another photo we are with our mother. Snow-covered wooden skis lean against a fence. Peter is kneeling on a sled that looks very much like the one that now lies in our backyard here in Vermont, abandoned by our grandchildren after Christmas, now exposed by a January thaw. And here we are again, on a hay wagon with our mother, our pants and boots snow-covered. Where did we get the proper clothes for this climate, fresh from Florida as we were? Paddy wears two different hats. One is blue, tying under the chin and has a standup semi circular crown. The other is white and furry and encircles her face and also ties under her chin. We are wearing little coats that button up the front. Peter's coat has a velvet collar. We don't look cold. We do have hats on our heads.

We are nearly five years old and attend Margaret's one room school-house. I sit on the front bench with Peter beside me. Margaret told Paddy that Peter was surprisingly smart for his age. Nothing was said about me as far as I remember. My memories and my mother's stories now begin to merge in my mind. She would recount an event of our shared past, beginning with "Do you remember when...." And I could say that I remembered. "Do you remember when the chimney caught on fire?" Margaret is at school, Tom is not on the farm, and the house chimney erupts in flames. My mother asks Peter to run down to the schoolhouse and tell Margaret, but he is too frightened. Desperately she turns to me. She loved to tell how I sped down the road on my little legs, braids flying, carrying the news. All my life I have responded to news of fresh disaster with the belief that I must take action.

Imminent rescue is up to me. Not for nothing did I become a professional social worker, subduing the mental fires of the psychiatrically disturbed.

I must get to the incident in the barn, though this is a memory I wish to avoid. I did avoid it for most of my life, so much so that when my mother asked me over the years if I did remember, I lied and said I didn't. It happened because I loved the barn and the cows. I treated those animals like pets and good-heartedly gave them extra salt licks, though Tom kindly admonished me for that. It was not good for the cows.

There was a hired hand in the barn, a young man whom I apparently followed slavishly. The long and the short of it is that one day, Paddy, react-ing to a sixth sense, came out to the barn from the house just in time. The hired hand had me on the hay with my pants down. Why was it so hard to tell my mother that I did remember? Of course it was shame, coupled with my fear that I had done something terribly wrong. Perhaps I really liked him, and the result of my affection was "a very bad happening." Perhaps I was a lonely child missing her abruptly vanished father and here was a young man, maybe close to his age, who seemed interested in me. He zeroed in on my vulnerability. None of this was ever talked about that I can remember. But he was immediately fired. Those generous people, Tom and Margaret, must have felt terrible that this could have happened when they were trying so hard to do good.

Much later in life, my husband I became friends with a young dairy farmer in our Vermont village. Visits to his barn remind me of all the good things about the months at the Wyatt farm. The rancid smell of sileage brings the good memories, not only of the farm in Bethel but of other barns I knew in the summers of my Minnesota childhood. Yet I find our friend's hired man disturbing. I am reminded of what happened so long ago. I have learned enough about the seamy underside of rural life in these beautiful hills to know that it could happen here and now.

We can't stay at the farm any longer. This may not have been the only reason but it surely was a precipitant to our inevitable departure. But where to go? Paddy wants to go back to England. Margaret finds an article in the St. Paul newspaper noting that a British Consulate is opening there. The new British Consul has recently arrived. Perhaps he can help. Paddy writes him, describing her plight and desire to return home. For the past three years, she has had to depend on her courage, her ingenuity, and the kindness of others. The war keeps her here on the wrong side of the Atlantic. She wants a solution.

The British Consul replies that there is nothing he can do to get her back to England. He seems kind, however, and she takes a leap. She thanks him for his reply, tactfully notes that perhaps he has typed his own letter and asks if he needs a secretary in his new office. His name is Leo Lamb and he answers. He writes that he is presently interviewing a young woman, as he has begun to staff his office, but if she wants to see him, he would be happy to meet with her.

He hires her, for he sees that she has secretarial skills, charm, and intelligence.

He offers her the post of Clerical Assistant with a salary of $120 a month in the St. Paul office of the British Consulate, to begin Monday, May 3rd, 1943. Here is his letter to her, dated 28th. April 1943, addressed to Mrs. P. Vaughan, c/o Mrs. Wyatt, Bethel, Minn. "The duties include receiptionist (sic) work in the main public office, typing, filing, and any other similar work which it may be necessary for you to perform. The office is open to the public from 9 a.m. to noon, and from 2 p.m. to 4 p.m., on week days, and from 9 a.m. to noon on Saturdays, but the actual working hours would usually be longer than that, and if called upon you would be expected to work on Sundays and holidays without overtime. Such occasions would under normal conditions be infrequent."

He is a knight in shining armor, on full gallop from the British Foreign Office, recently arrived in this strange little outpost of Empire in the American Midwest.

How surprising that after all the travels and wanderings in this foreign land, ultimately it is her own country that comes to Paddy's rescue. Saved we are. She has a job and an income and a modicum of security.

CHAPTER 9

Life Begins in St. Paul

WE MOVE INTO TOWN AND take up residence on the upper floor of a duplex on Portland Avenue. Paddy has met someone who knows someone named Bud who was living here with his wife until she fled back to New York, for reasons that eventually become more clear. The actual owner of the duplex is the man's father, who agrees to rent it to Paddy for $50 a month. She must pay utilities. Tom and Margaret Wyatt recommend Edith to be our live in child care person. She comes with us from Bethel. We need her now that Paddy is going to work. I have always thought of her as "mentally challenged" but I don't know that she actually was. More likely, she was a simple farm woman, reluctantly recruited into city life for the promise of five dollars a week. She spends many hours sitting at the kitchen table, clad in a cotton housedress, arms crossed over her large shapeless torso. Edith finds us very difficult, often telling us that we are "bad eggs," and we don't do much to disabuse her of this notion. I remember Peter kicking her.

The duplex apartment has two bedrooms, a little one at the end of the hallway for Edith and the master two bedded room for Peter and me. Paddy sleeps on a daybed in the dining room. Two sisters occupy the downstairs apartment. They are dark haired and foreign. They drink their coffee made from cans labeled "Kaffee Klatch," a name which, in my child's mind, confirms their foreign mysteriousness. Perhaps they are refugees, though not "evacuees" like us.

Over time, I have developed the notion that being an evacuee is more socially acceptable than being a refugee. Evacuees are a kind of elite of those temporarily dispossessed of country.   Evacuees can go back home eventually, though we never did. Refugees probably never could.   As I have told my story over the years, it has seemed more elegant to be an evacuee. It smacks less of desperation and permanent uprootedness, less alien. As a five year old child I was aware of none of this.   My only serious cultural challenge growing up in Minnesota was how to manage the strangeness of my name.   I am convinced that there was no one named "Felicity" west of the Appalachians and certainly not in Minnesota.   I struggled to explain that I was not "Phyllis," nor was I a sister of Faith, Hope, and Charity.   One day, riding the streetcar home from school, I just gave up and told a nice lady, who asked, that my name was "Jane."

The foreign sisters depart and a family moves in with two little boys. Benny Story is younger than we are.   He distinguishes himself in our eyes one day by appearing stark naked in their downstairs living room window. Life gets even more interesting when the "someone" who is our landlord materializes as an actual person --tall, handsome, dark-haired.   He comes to our room one night as we are propped up in our matching twin beds, beds for twins.   He peers at us and politely apologizes as he retrieves some clothes from the closet.   Eventually, he comes around more and more.   He is called "Bud" and he and Paddy begin a romance or an affair.   What is the difference?   Licit versus illicit, perhaps.   Paddy is still married to our father in England, but time, distance, and war have stretched those bonds to the breaking point. The father void in our lives persists.   It appears now that a candidate to fill it is showing up for duty.

As we get to know Bud's relatives, we are accruing an extended family. His sister, Mary, her husband, Bill and their three boys live at the other end of our block. One son is our age, another only a year and a half younger.   Mary teaches me to make a bed with neatly folded corners. I liked this, I remember, and still take pleasure in doing it exactly right.   Bud's parents, gentle folk who moved to Minnesota from Virginia at the turn of the century, also live nearby. His mother comes by the apartment one day with her Swedish maid, Lydia, to look at the furnishings. They seem particularly interested in the long, low Chinese table in the living room.   Perhaps it belongs to her and she considers taking it away. But the table stays. Maybe she is really on a scouting mission, curious about this little wandering family who have arrived, homeless and without references.

But what about Bud? It is a lot easier to digress into his family background than to take up this challenge. How do you write about someone who could make life miserable -- but who had great gifts which he shared with us? Paddy always claimed that she loved him. She may have really believed that she could get him to give up, or "control," his drinking. Over time the result was that she drank too much herself. He never could stop. The term "on the wagon" became common in our house, those fantasies in which alcoholics indulge to convince themselves that they are not actually alcoholics. If you can stop for a while, surely you are in control. We were also living in a time when only street bums were "alcoholics." Genteel upper middle class people who drank "cocktails" at regularly prescribed hours, known to us children as "'tini time," could surely never be called alcoholics or drunks. Bud's problem, however, exceeded even the very lax boundaries around drinking that existed in their social set.

Bud is a journalist, a talented writer, who had a byline on the final front page of the once famous "New York World." Under its owner, Joseph Pulitzer, the World became known for its sensationalism, newly termed "yellow journalism." This page, issued on the paper's final day in February, 1931, was framed and hung in our home. Bud has many stories to tell of his New York days. He and his Midwestern friends flocked to the speakeasies of Greenwich Village for more excitement than staid St. Paul could offer. These were the years of F. Scott Fitzgerald, a native of St. Paul, whom everyone, including Bud, claimed to have known. In my mind's eye, I can still see Fitzgerald's Summit Avenue row house, now in the National Register of Historic Places. We pass it often in our comings and goings on Summit Hill. Hence we could say to others that we almost knew him as well.

By the time we meet Bud, he is in his early forties, settled into a reporter's job at the "St. Paul Dispatch," located on 4th Street, near City Hall and the local favorite Irish bar. The "newspaper," as we called it, is an exciting place. For starters, you could stand outside the building and watch the whirling presses through the window as they turned out the daily paper. Even better, we had early seats at disaster news before it turned up in print. Unfortunately, Bud's work day often ended up in the bar which meant he would be well into his cups by the time he got home.

Over the years, things get worse. One night the police arrive at our house to take him into custody after he has driven into parked cars on his way home. By now I am a teenager. Though I have blocked it from my memory, my mother told me that I was the only one who could persuade him to go with the police in their patrol car. Once when I said I didn't remember, she replied that I probably didn't want to. I became very good at crisis management. And I always knew when he was drunk. It had something to do with the slackness of his lips, the unfocussed look in his eyes, and a particular hand gesture that involved a stroking of his lower jaw.

But what of his gifts? He taught me to drive a car and to drive well. I was behind the wheel on a maiden voyage on a seldom-traveled Minnesota country road. Bud was in the passenger seat, reading a newspaper. He later admitted that he just couldn't imagine that anyone didn't know how to drive. When I nearly veered off the road, then he had to pay attention. He passed on a lot of vehicular wisdom which I still retain. If you see a small animal, like a dog or a cat or even a bird, in the middle of the road, he said, never, ever swerve to avoid it. It is better to hit the small animal than lose control of the car and end up as the victim in your own accident. Grip the steering wheel tightly and drive on through. Years later, my husband, with me as passenger, veered to avoid a cat. Our little red VW did a full rotation while travelling upside down in the middle of the road, landing upright, fenders crushed inside the wheels and leaving a bright red streak on the highway. Fortunately, it was not our blood. Had I been driving I would have chosen to hit the cat. I know it. I was that well trained.

Bud taught me to swim. Or rather, he knew I could swim-- but I didn't. He saw that I refused to let go of the dock as I ventured into the water. I just kept paddling back and forth in my own self-created safe space. Finally, he picked me up and threw me off the end of the dock into water over my head. It worked! I swam untethered for the first time in my life. I was nine years old. I still swim. It is my favorite form of exercise.

He was a reader and a writer who forcefully imparted his favorite grammatical bugbears whenever he had the chance. He would pounce on an unwitting culprit with his orthodoxy. This often occurred at the dinner table. The incorrect use of "like" instead of "as." "I walked down the road like he did." It must be "I walked down the road as he did." "The way he did" would also be acceptable. Also, you cannot and must not use "real" as an adverb. "She looked real nice." Wrong again. It must be "she looked really nice." "Real" is merely an adjective. It has no meaningful relationship to a verb. How he would cringe today to see his bugbears enshrined in common usage.

Bud was handsome. Here is a portrait, probably taken by his friend, Paul, a photographer at the paper. He is seated in half profile. We see him only from the waist up, his right elbow resting on his knee, a cigarette casually held in his right hand between the index and middle fingers. A wisp of smoke drifts across the black background. He is wearing a light-colored heavy cloth jacket over a soft shirt. The cuff is soiled and his checked knit tie falls in a rumpled way to his waist, a carelessly done tribute to a necessity of dress. His black hair is perfectly cut, brushed smoothly back from his forehead. There is an impending widow's peak as his hairline is beginning to recede. His features are even, his nose classical and straight, his lips well-carved. He gazes into the distance, somewhere beyond the cigarette, and his face bears an expression of sullenness, even sensuality. There is a sadness here, even before alcohol fully claimed his liver and cigarettes killed his lungs.

But, for now he has fallen in love with our mother and they marry during the summer when we are nine. They fly to Sioux Falls, South Dakota, in order to do this. Somehow Paddy has managed to divorce our father, at least enough to satisfy legal requirements in South Dakota. They had approached a friend, a prominent St. Paul attorney, about the divorce. He said he couldn't do it, but referred them to a less notable lawyer on West 7th Street who could probably arrange it. Their friend possibly knew too much of the law.

In the meantime, Paddy has settled into her job at the Consulate, a career woman ahead of her time. Over the years, I was the only one among my schoolmates whose mother worked outside the home. This didn't seem remarkable to me, but I admit there were times when I wished she were home making BLTs for lunch like my friend Nancy's mother. My mother's office was on the 16th floor of the First National Bank building in downtown St. Paul. Room 1662, to be exact. The Bank building was the tallest in town, a midwestern skyscraper. Its only regional competition was the Foshay Tower in downtown Minneapolis which now is merely a mini Washington monument in the company of giants. The Bank building remains a unique presence in the St. Paul skyline, topped by its enormous 1ST sign in neon.

By the time I was nine, I was old enough to take the streetcar downtown after school by myself to meet my mother after work for errands or shopping. I was instructed to stand on the corner where she could see me from her office window. I was never to cross the street until she came to get me. One day I arrived on the corner as usual and waited for her. I waited and waited. Then I waited some more. I have no idea how long I stood there, dutifully not crossing the street. Finally, I had no recourse. I crossed. I entered the lobby of the building and saw the familiar elevator man who knew me. "Your mother has already left." The next thing I remember was being back home at the kitchen table eating my favorite meal, creamed chipped beef on toast.

She had forgotten that I was coming that day. There had been many frantic phone calls. A neighbor, an attorney with an office downtown, had seen me standing on the corner. St. Paul was a little village then where everyone knew everyone. "Downtown" was small and compact and most people worked within a few blocks of each other. A rescue party was sent out, though I don't remember much about it. It was really quite a terrible event. My mother was filled with remorse and never forgot it. Trust in my little world took another hit. I still get very anxious if someone doesn't show up as expected. And I am always on time.

The Consulate was a small family, staffed by Paddy, another secretary and the Consul. The Consuls came and went throughout my growing up years. They were single, or married, or had children or didn't. Leo Lamb was the first, the one who put Paddy on her feet. Some were more exotic than others. They had come from previous Foreign Office postings, dribbled throughout the shrinking Empire. St. Paul was a far cry from Marrakesh where the wife of one Consul was said to have been a painting companion of Winston

Churchill. In my mind's eye I see them seated on a hillside together with their canvases and brushes. Later, a single man arrived in St. Paul with his live-in Swiss housekeeper. Eyebrows were raised but, of course, nothing was said. These men had an aristocratic bent, very Foreign Office, very cultured, with one exception. It was he who felt it was his duty to stand in the doorway of the open walk in safe when I came to the office. This was presumably intended to protect deep secrets of the Empire from thieving little hands. Or maybe to absolve him from any future accusations of breaches of security protocol. Who knows? He just seemed different, a bit of a fish out of water in what was, by now, my extensive experience of British Consuls. Perhaps he was not of the better classes.

CHAPTER 10

Settled Down

WE HAVE WANDERED FOR THREE years: Oxford to London, boat train from London's Euston station to "destination unknown" protected by acts of wartime secrecy. It became Glasgow and the "Duchess of York" and a convoy of 40 ships heading at top speed for Halifax. Montreal, then New York to Johnson City. Tennessee, a little gatehouse. Florida by the beach. Minnesota farm in the depths of winter. Breathless journey. War story. Now landed.

I never thought my mother was one for self reflection. I believed she had no inclination. She certainly didn't have the time. So far, she has been the central character in our story. Peter and I are along for the ride. I am now allowed to wonder how she managed. Did she despair? Was she frightened? How stiff was her upper lip? What of terrors? What feelings and what fears were locked away in little closets in her brain? Throughout her life, she harbored an ever-present sense of impending danger. Often, while riding in a car and, in anticipation of non accidents to come, she would noisily suck in her breath and press her feet hard to the floor- boards. The driver could be unnerved to a point of real danger. When we passed a logging truck on the Interstate, she was sure the truck would heave over as we went by and crush us in a wooden death. There is a turn in our little dirt road in Vermont that she was always sure, as we drove out, that I would miss. We could careen down through the pasture and meet our end in the neighbor's vegetable garden.

I saw all this in her later years. As I grew up I only knew that she was never to be contradicted. "Don't contradict me." I was astonished when friends argued with their parents. I couldn't imagine it. Now I believe Paddy's iron lady grip was the way in which she kept control of her life. But pierce it, as I did many years later, and she came apart. It was not a pretty sight. I was visiting her in Minneapolis and we went to dinner at Ping's, her favorite Chinese restaurant, where she had charmed the waiter whose name was Grant ("Grahhnt" in her tones). I didn't like Ping's to begin with because they didn't give you fortune cookies. Too upscale for that. I was already in a bad mood. She had been pestering me all day about getting together with her stepdaughter, a woman about my age who had the same name in another form. She was Patti. I didn't dislike her but had no particular desire to see her during this visit. I don't think my mother stopped for a moment to think about my wishes. The agenda was hers. She defined it. If I didn't see Patti, Paddy wouldn't look good. And she must look good at all costs. Her narcissism was both her strength and her weakness. If you can roll over people and not look back, you can keep on going, until that moment when someone or something stops you in your tracks. It tears at the rigidly constructed but very fragile false self and leaves you defenseless.

I had had enough of her pushing this time. I lost it. Don't tread on me! I am not your social agent, here to give you status which you can't claim for yourself. British "school leaver" at fifteen versus Harvard graduate with a Master's degree. Not my fault! My daughter, as an adult, once said that she thought my mother was jealous of me. I don't remember exactly what I said at Ping's but I contradicted her, big time. Maybe I actually told her to stop pushing me. I could have. The balloon burst. The air went out of her. She dissolved into tears and became utterly undone, incoherent. I thrust the credit card receipt in front of her. She had to sign it, but that was all she could do. She stumbled out of the restaurant. Percy, my then stepfather, followed her. He was a very nice man, on the surface an innocent who never saw bad things happening in the world. I followed them. I was angry and wondered how I could ever speak to her again.

What had I done? Had I destroyed her? We returned to their condominium and I fled to my guest room downstairs. I wrote her an angry screed filled with recriminations. I unloaded a lifetime of resentments, too many to enumerate. I never gave it to her. The next morning, I had to go to their apartment for breakfast. She opened the door and greeted me as if nothing had happened. That's how she did it - as if nothing had happened. She moved on, ignoring the damage, that of her own making as well as that done to her by others. She stuffed the nastiness into those little closets and locked the doors behind her. This was how she coped.

Coped, she did, as she worked to build a life for us in St. Paul. But she had not been counting on falling in love. By the time three years had passed, she knew Bud's flaws. Here in my safe little home office where I write, I reach into a cluttered box of old photos, letters, news clippings - mine and hers - a very disorganized memory dump. If I believed in spirits, I would say that my hand was guided. Here are two letters, preserved in carbon copy, letters that I had missed in rummaging through her things after she died. She had written them to Bud, thirteen years between the letters. In 1946, she lays it out for him, calling it "Final Warning." "If we are going to marry and have a life together, you have to stop your drinking, stop your ambling. You know I will be by your side." Her words, straight out of country Western but genuinely felt and poignantly written. "If you cannot do this," she continues, "I will make my own plans. I would go back to England so that Tom could pay for the childrens' education and "see them from time to time." So we do have a father after all. We surely didn't know it.

A year later, his and her divorces final, they marry. Either he has tried a new mode of living or she has capitulated. Maybe both. The marriage doesn't work but it takes a long time to play itself out. Thirteen years later, in 1959, she writes again because it is impossible to talk to him. He is always "tight" when she gets home from work, or he is asleep, or out at the bar. It is her "Dear John" letter, a plea for a better future which she must grasp before it is too late. She fears his destructive influence. She is "cowed and frustrated." She sees herself becoming more like him and his drunken friends. She suggests they try living apart and finds him an apartment nearby on Grand Avenue. He leaves.

Our story, however, has gone forward too quickly. Let us rewind to our little world on Portland Avenue. We may be comfortably settled down, but the rest of the world is there in backdrop and just within reach. In April, 1945,

President Roosevelt dies in Warm Springs, Georgia. I am only seven years old but I store the memory of that day. That August, a nuclear *coup de grace* obliterates two Japanese cities. The war is over. We children parade around the neighborhood banging pots and pans in celebration. Paddy continues to send food packages "home" to England, featuring Spam and other canned luxuries. My English cousin, Kay, a few years younger than me, wears my hand-me-down dresses. She lives in Oxford and calls them her "American dresses." Her father is Paddy's brother, Len, who can play the piano by ear. There is no word from our father, at least to my ears. He recedes into the distance as the war recedes. He goes off the page. Blank screen.

School and Home

PETER AND I BEGIN FIRST grade at Irving School. We have milk at recess and I get trapped in a house of blocks built by the other children. There I meet my future stepcousin, Bruce, who has a horrible black patch under one lens of his glasses because of an eye problem. He is the ringleader. The school building is very old and closes after two years because of a broken furnace.

We need another school. Bud makes sure that we don't go to our district school. It is in the wrong part of town and is not attended by the "right kind" of children. He is behaving like a father. Good education matters. It also matters very much to our mother who left school when she was 15 for lack of money for her to continue. Paddy meets the esteemed headmaster of the local boys' private school at a cocktail party and she takes another leap. She charms him and, before the evening is out, he has offered Peter a special scholarship for evacuee boys. He may have invented it on the spot, riven by her poignant story. Who wouldn't be? Peter begins the St. Paul Academy in second grade. He wears the required navy blue sweater with two gold stripes around the arms denoting his grade, which Paddy had knit for him.

But what of me? I am off to public school, Linwood, travelling by street-car and foot through the fifth grade. I learn to read and write and color between the lines. The scarlet tanager is red with black wings. I hold my first ball point pen and I see my first jet plane from the window of my fifth grade classroom. I write in cursive, making long lines of connected loops known as the Palmer Method. In this way, everyone's handwriting is identical which was, it seemed, desirable. In the third grade I get my first Valentine from the boy of my dreams. He is very cute and has lots of black hair and sits behind me in the last row. I am put in the boys' line while we are lining up to go into school because my jacket is the boys' color, army khaki. After that embarrassment, I make sure my braids are visible outside my hood. I want a jacket like the other girls, with pink flowers embroidered on the dark brown wool. At some level I am beginning to sense that I may be different from these Midwestern children.

My mother, however, was not content with my school arrangement. In those days it was not uncommon, even among well to do educated families, to send the boy to private school and the daughter to the public school. Why spend money educating her when she would end up marrying and not need all that learning? Not so for our mother. She was a working woman and, throughout her life, she was painfully aware of her own limited education.

Summit School for Girls was founded in 1917 as an independent but corollary school to St. Paul Academy. The indomitable headmistress, Sarah Converse, had been there at the founding in 1917. She was still there in 1948 when I was ten and due to enter sixth grade. Fearlessly, Paddy takes me to her. Mercifully, Miss Converse deems me an acceptable child. She states that she would do for me what John DeQuedville Briggs is doing for Peter. In other words, she offers pretty much a free ride.

Miss Converse wore a pince nez. Her hair was styled in a cap of orderly descending waves which ended at the nape of her neck. She was a presence. She presided over a faculty of intelligent, educated women who gave their lives to better ours. I realize now that they were all single. Was it required that they not have entanglements of family that would distract them from their mission? They were Miss Colby (Math), Miss Walsh (Latin and Spanish), Miss Spicer (English), Miss Stevie (Chemistry and Biology), Miss Busyn (History), Mam'selle Diebold (French), Miss Kelly (Piano), Miss Gunsolly (Gym). I love Summit School. I am safe there. If home is unreliable in this regard, school is not. I flourish. I do well academically, I star in school plays. I am Emily in Our Town. Julie in Liliom. I sing in the Acapella Summit Singers. I become Class President. I make life long friends.

At home family life takes on a semblance of stability, fragile though it may be. We move to a house on Fairmont Avenue, which Paddy and Bud have bought for $10,000. I have my own room and Peter has his. There is an upstairs playroom where we gather with our friends. Here Bud and Peter array armies of lead soldiers in battle formation on the pingpong table. The Cameron Highlanders, the Black Watch. Bud knows them all, inherited from his own childhood. A piano appears and is lifted through an upstairs window. I begin lessons and play "The Tennessee Waltz" in a recital. The war is over but there is still no word of our father, the missing man. I never think to ask the question. It is as if there is no question to ask.

We go to the grandparents, Bud's parents, for Thanksgiving, Christmas and birthdays. There are 11 of us, his sister Mary and her husband Bill, their sons, Bruce, Blair, and Billy, Grandmother and Grandfather, and the four of us. Lydia, the Swedish maid, prepares and serves the meal, passing on the left and taking away from the right. Grandmother was from Virginia, from gentlefolk, educated mannerly people, lawyers and teachers. Her Minnesota household reflects her upbringing. There are small crystal finger bowls between courses, with bits of lemon floating in the water. Grandfather carves. It is either turkey, eye of the round or a whole roast of beef, depending on the occasion. Grandmother signals Lydia for change of courses by pressing a button on the floor with her foot that rings a bell in the kitchen. As soon as we arrive at their house, we children rush to the attic to play the ancient pinball machine. It is "Baseball," a game under glass. You pull back a lever and let it go. It whacks a metal ball which is then propelled around a painted baseball diamond. There are holes at the bases and tiny upstanding spokes scattered here and there to deflect the ball. You hold your breath, hoping your ball at least makes it around first base. Maybe all the way to home plate. No skill involved here, just plain luck. Downstairs, the grownups drink their martinis in the living room and talk politics in gradually escalating voices.

We dress up for these occasions. I am the only girl so there is no competition in the clothes department. I don't have closets full of clothes but those I have are nice. My mother is passing her good taste on to me. She wants me to be well turned out, a visible credit to her. It must have pleased her that I was a fairly good looking child. Not pretty in the blonde Minnesota Scandinavian way, but nonetheless attractive. She found a dressmaker to make my first "formal" for a school dance. It was light blue satin and strapless. The skirt was covered with a single layer of white organdy and there was a little matching organdy jacket. She took me for fittings. It was a beautiful thing and I felt very special.

Lydia always makes an angel food cake for the birthday person. She spreads it meticulously with boiled white frosting and decorates it with little red cinnamon hearts. Could it be that each grownup had one, too? In my first year at college, away from home, I even wondered if Lydia could get a cake to me in time for my mid December birthday. I knew she couldn't, but nonetheless I wished and wondered. It is hard to imagine the Grandparents without Lydia. In fact, they never were without her. Grandfather died in his eighties and only then did Grandmother allow Lydia to move from her room in the attic to the second floor. She needed her close by. There she stayed until Grandmother died.

CHAPTER 12

The River

WE GO "OUT TO THE river" in the summer. Most people in Minnesota go "up to the lake" but we do better than that. After all, a lake is static. It just sits there. You look at it and it looks back. In contrast, a river is so much more. It flows. It comes from somewhere on its way to somewhere else. It will carry you along. Or you can defy it, put your paddle in the water and head upstream. It is never the same from one moment to the next. You cannot capture it. You must learn its ways. When you swim across, you target a spot on the opposite shore well above where you actually want to land. In this way, the current becomes your friend. You turn its negative force to your advantage. You do not get lost in its power and drift downstream against your will.

Every summer our tripartite extended family deploys into three houses on the Minnesota side of the St. Croix river, four miles north of the village of Marine-on-the-St. Croix. Mary and Bill and the boys have the Green House. Next to them, going north, is the Grandparents' house, a creamy yellow frame. Our modest white bungalow, Bud's house, with a big screen porch across the entire front, is further along a small road. A telephone party line links us on land and the river connects us offshore. There are other houses down the line, homes of our friends who, like us are released from the boredom and perils of summer in the city. Our parents fear polio, which emerges every year in this season, making the city unsafe. We leave town.

We are free at last. These are the days of joy and boats and woods and the wild river. The Soo Line runs between the Twin Cities and Sault Ste Marie. The tracks pass nearby and the hooting whistle of the engine marks our summer days. We listen for the 2.20, eager to leave our houses after a parent controlled midday break. Return to your boats, crank your outboard motors into purring life, head for the sandbar and the village of willows you are building there. Go swimming, stay in the water until your eyes are blurry and you feel like a fish.

Or a boat trip upstream this afternoon? We know how to miss the wing dams just under the surface of the water, rock dams that can shear an outboard cotter pin. We know the language of the channel markers, big white X's mounted on trees. There are caves up there beyond the high railroad trestle that crosses the river. Had Indians lived in these caves? On the way, we stop at the trestle and make a challenge to gravity. We climb to the top of the wooden pilings on either side, nearly as high as the bridge itself. We jump, falling into the water below. My gut wrenches as I plummet. I can do it, boys, even though I am a girl, your sister, your cousin, your friend. But no one can match Hutch, who climbs to the very top of the trestle itself. He drops, a slender summer-browned boy, and breaks the river's surface, his feet knifing the water below.

The whistle of the 9.20 sends us home at night. We walk barefoot along darkened roads and the riverside paths between the houses. Perhaps we had been playing cards in Grandmother's summer house, a small brown frame cottage next to her vegetable garden. Or maybe I had left the boys for an evening and joined my friend Alice at her piano as we sang our way through <u>The Fireside Book of Folk Songs.</u> For Bonnie Annie Laurie I'd lay me doon and dee. In Dublin's fair city where girls are so pretty lives Sweet Molly Malone. Loch Lomond's Braes are bonny! On another evening we might be down at the Lewises. This was a much more frightening walk home, longer, on even darker roads. Or we might have ventured no farther than Grandmother's, where she has the cribbage board out on the card table. We settle in with the current "New Yorker," flipping the pages to find the cartoons.

Our River life builds a magical home in my heart. One dark night as I walked back home I wondered to myself what the man I would marry was doing now. I had no shortage of boyfriends in my dating life but I didn't think of them this way. They were just "dates." I met my husband at college a few years later. He had spent his summers on a lake in Northern New Jersey. There was no river --which can be forgiven. The rest I understood immediately. There were three family homes, his own with his parents and siblings, his aging grandmother next door, and his aunt, uncle, and cousins were on the other side. It was surely magic. We had already lived a part of each others' lives.

CHAPTER 13
Retrieval

WHAT HAPPENED TO YOUR FATHER? People ask this question when I talk of my memoir, this writing. It is my habit to say just enough to stir a little interest. But not too much, for words disappear into the air once they are spoken. I fear that if I say too much I will somehow lose my story. I write to protect it, to give it permanence. I am creating my own narrative, my own truth. Yet sadly I find truth lacking. It is only a roughly-made patchwork of bits and pieces, snatches of remembrance and invention. But there is no whole cloth,

How could he have sent you away? His children. Did he love you? I hear the subtext when they ask the question. I rationalize, construct, reconstruct. History is my defense. I cite Dunkirk. Fear drives impulsive decisions, I say. He did cry for us when he saw our train leaving Euston Station. But I don't really know. How can I know?

As I weave this tale of mine, I wonder what I will do to answer these compelling questions. Why the void, why the complete loss of contact with him? As far as I knew there was nothing. Nothing. My listeners find this puzzling, too. War is one thing, but the war ended, they say. What happened then? I cannot "go there" because for me there is nowhere to go. Until last week, for I have found treasure.

All winter I had been bedeviled by the mess in the entryway of my house. I have promised myself that, when spring comes, I will dig in and sort. The front entry is for coats, hats, and mittens. Drop your boots and winter shoes here on the tile floor before you climb the few stairs to the living area of the house. There is a spool bench if you need to sit down. The bench belonged to

Grandmother. She kept it in the sunroom of her Kenwood Parkway home in St. Paul. Turn to the right before you mount the stairs and you find yourself in the back half of the vestibule. There is a coat closet on your left and an unused door to the outside which is blocked by a small secretary, a writing desk. Paddy's desk. The corner space between the secretary and the right hand wall has become a convenient repository for "mother's stuff." There is a box labeled, "Paddy letters – Save." Another box, a liquor store castoff, shouts, "Paddy – Personal – Letters – Keep" in my handwriting. I had sealed it with brown packaging tape. When did I pack this? Was it during her move from Minneapolis to Hanover, New Hampshire, in 1999? Perhaps it was later, when I cleared her possessions after her death in 2006. Keep looking and you will see Paddy's portfolio from her days at art school in Oxford, which she attended during her teens. I have sorted through the still lifes, the calligraphy, and the watercolors several times over the years. I can't throw them out, but I don't know what to do with them. Who could have brought this large, awkward brown cracked carrying case across the Atlantic? Surely it could not have accompanied us on our wartime journey. The boxes, the portfolio, random framed pictures and photos have been here for so long that I no longer see them. But lately the mess has been getting on my nerves. At summer's beginning, around Memorial Day, I decide it is time to dig, clear, and clean.

Meanwhile, as my writing progresses, I realize that I can no longer avoid bringing Tom Vaughan, my father, to the fore. I must create a space for him here and fill in the blanks as best I can. He is like the father in a family of paper dolls. Cut out his clothes from the pages of the book. Leave the tabs intact, turn them down over his shoulders and attach the clothes to the Father doll. But this is a father in two dimensions. How can I clothe him here? How can I give him flesh? How do I answer the annoying questions that people ask?

One morning, as I tire of writing and thinking, I go to the vestibule to work. I pull stuff from the corner -- all the familiar stuff. I resolve to get rid of some of it once and for all. Paddy is gone and that's that. But what is this large white wrinkly plastic bag? There is a logo on one side in red, yellow, and brown stating that "Pepperidge Farm Remembers..." A bread company remembers what, I wonder. On the reverse is a list of Midwest stores including one in Minneapolis at 4503 France Avenue South. I want to get a better look. It is heavy and full. I drag it over to the spool bench and sit down. I open it. It is filled with letters -- dozens and dozens of letters. I reach in and pick out a few. I start to read them. It doesn't take long before I realize that what I have in my hands are letters from my father to my mother, letters he wrote to her immediately after our departure, spanning the war years. I am stunned. I have never seen these letters. I did not know of their existence. How can I have missed them in all the packings, unpackings and sortings of many moves in many years? I delve deeper and pull out handfuls. I scan and read some more. I pile them around me on the bench and on the floor. Pile after pile. I see that these are not just a few casual letters, but a steady stream of connection, flowing from my father's pen and typewriter, weekly, daily at times, to his absent wife and children. He uses both sides of the paper to keep within the weight limits of wartime mail. The letters slip easily through my fingers and the paper is still strong. The handwritten ones are on thicker paper, neat and readable in black or blue ink. The return address is that of my Grandma Vaughan, where my father lived after we left. The Bungalow, Lyndworth Close, Headington, Oxford. The house is at the end of the Close, a few doors down from Number 7, our own house that we had left so suddenly.

Everything in this bag is a jumble. There are not only letters from my father, but from many others as well -- all men, except for those from Paddy's mother and father. There are at least fifty letters from Bernard, a former lover, who was also a friend of Tom, our father. Bernard's wartime return address is 939735 Bdr. B. Poole, c/o The Stormy Petrel, Tern Hill, Market Drayton, Shropshire. It is his mother's home. He writes, "I find that Standing Orders lay down that one does not send military addresses abroad, but instead gives an address from which a reply can be forwarded – hence the above. " His actual wartime location cannot be disclosed. He writes to Paddy from 1940 to 1944. In a final letter, he declares that loving her was a mistake, that she is making a wreck of her life, and that she will never find the perfect man. This is a long way from "Darling Paddy, I kiss you," of earlier letters.

Geoffrey Moody, also from Oxford and a close friend of both Tom and Paddy, kept in touch with her for many years and she with him. During the war he is stationed with India Command, 15/1 Punjab Regiment. In 1943 he writes of his experience there.

"I have seen the snows of the Himaalias, not Himalayers, from a hundred miles away, a white cliff along the edge of the sky over the hot plains. I've seen every Hindu house outlined in little oil lamps for Diwali – I've listened, the only Englishman within twenty miles, to the Mohammedans praying to Allah at the beginning of the month of fasting. I've driven incredible old lorries up and down the Grand Trunk Road – I've seen Kim's Zam-Zammah in Lahore, the Red Fort in Delhi. I've lived on native food and known what it feels like to have a complete village turn out to look at you. I've seen blue bottle flies over the incredible green of growing rice, I've heard the noise the parrots make in the trees, I've shuddered (and still do) when the jackals shriek in chorous (sic) like souls out of hell. I like whisky – but have only been a little tight once when my friends decided I ought to be on my 30ᵗʰ birthday – I climbed to the roof of the mess and poured a jug of water over them. I can speak Urdu fairly, and can understand Punjabi. I have on shorts and a topi and I am as nearly Anglo-Indian in my natural speech as you, my dear Paddy, are sadly American in your writing. "

I love Geoffrey's writing, for I have also lived in India. I have seen the white cliffs of the Himalayas, from the window of a Royal Nepal Airlines DC-3, in 1964. I have seen the lights of Divali and have been the object of the stares of villagers. I have heard jackals and panthers shriek in the night. I have become nearly Anglo-Indian in my skin color and in the cadence of my speech.

There are more letters. They come from someone named Frank, an American, stationed in Fort Gordon, Georgia. There are letters from Lynn Baldwin, from Tennessee and Jacksonville, in the Navy, who now has a San Francisco APO address. He thinks he can marry her. Her brother Arthur writes from India during the war where he too is stationed with India

Command.   Her mother, my grandma, in Oxford writes to "My dear Lily, Peter and Felicity."

My vestibule clean-up campaign grinds to a halt. I sit on the bench surrounded by all this paper from the past. I am in serious disarray, inside and out. There is no order here. I find a basket on a nearby shelf. Here is an empty shoebox, too. I use them for temporary storage, assigning letters at random to one or the other. I am transported into a past, which until now, has been closed to me. The hours of my day of discovery slip by and too soon it is time for dinner and the husband. Reluctantly I break free from my cocoon of letters.

Part II

CHAPTER 14

Into My Father's World

MY PRESENT LIFE LAYS ITS claims on me. I am drawn into myriad entertaining trips, visits from friends and family obligations that cannot be ignored. The permissiveness of slow summer days occasionally softens the frantic pace. I leave the letters in the basket and shoebox. It is weeks before I make my move. Finally, responding to an impulse to organize, I gather up the shoebox, the basket, and the Pepperidge Farm bag, which still contains many letters.

I have an office upstairs in our house. It is a small, bright and quiet place. From the large window I can see beyond our woods as far as the Green Mountains to the west. Soon I have covered much of the floor around my desk with piles of letters. Perhaps I should sort them by writer. I stuff all Bernard's letters into one bulging envelope. Geoffrey and Frank's are joined in another. I separate those from Paddy's brother Arthur, written from England and others he sent later from his wartime post in India Command. A few letters are from her brother in law, Peter Vaughan, an officer in the Royal Navy who was stationed in Portsmouth during the war. There are letters from her family to her, both during the war and afterward.

The mother lode, however, is the correspondence from my father. Soon I realize I need more space on the floor piles. I need a table, a long one. I go to our garage and, with help from my ever-willing husband, we carry an ancient folding metal table up to the spare bedroom. It is a little tricky to open the table to its full length. The folding parts have become arthritic and complaining. They protest with metallic squeaks as we force them into place, but we succeed. I cover it with a faded India print tablecloth I had bought many years ago in a Delhi market place. It is the perfect surface upon which to array the letters of my Calcutta born father.

I begin. The only plan that seems to makes sense is to lay the letters out in chronological order. There are many. The first letter is handwritten in dark blue ink on light blue paper. It is dated European style 13.8.4 with the month in the middle. He wrote immediately after our departure, as we travelled from England to Canada and then on to Johnson City, Tennessee. My organizational plan goes into holding pattern. I must read the letter. Here, at long last, is my father's voice:

My darling, I wonder if you'll find this waiting for you when you arrive. I hope so but somehow I don't think its possible what with censorship delays and so on. Anyhow here's hoping. Your mother is writing too – it would be nice to have them both waiting for you – and nice for us to think that you would be arriving to something familiar, even if its only our handwriting.

I've been wondering very hard how you are getting on and exactly whereabouts, what you are doing, and how the babes like the "big boat," what was the railway trip like? I do hope they were good and slept well and that you were able to get some rest too.

That must sound like ancient history to you. By the time you get this letter you'll have been some thousand miles or so on American railways and seen negro Pullman porters, New York Central station, a skyscraper or two, been interviewed by reporters (or am I optimistic?) and in short have seen more new things than I bet you ever hoped or expected to see in your life.

And what has it been like on the boat? Were the babes on or off your hands most of the time? Was there a nice nursery? And (or perhaps I mustn't say it) did you meet any nice handsome young men?

I am asking for a lot I know darling, but I expect a day to day diary of your trip and I especially want to know the reaction of the Canadian and American public to attractive Mrs. Vaughan and the twins....I had a grand letter from Aunt Gwladys. She said "how brave of Paddy to set off across the world with those two children" — on the whole she seemed to approve…the grandmothers are both bearing up extremely well.

….Look after yourself my darling, enjoy yourself, don't worry, and think of me sometimes. Kiss the babes hard for me and ask them if they remember Tom who's at the office at this moment.

I find his cheerfulness unsettling. Does he think she's on a cruise? Or is he simply trying to make himself feel better in moments of remorse at what he has done? He wants her to enjoy herself and hopes there is a nursery on board. Never mind that this is war and a ship in our convoy ends up on the receiving end of a U-Boat torpedo. But how was he to know what we know now -- that this was an incredibly dangerous journey. For the time being I forgive his innocence, his youthful naivete. As I read on, the door to his world begins to open. In my mind's eye I imagine him. I think I can even hear his voice, as I heard it so many years later when I was grown. Perhaps it will be he who answers so many questions for me.

I pull away from reading, knowing that I must achieve some kind of order. I cannot continue my story until I find my way in. I spend hours. I look at each letter, noting its date and the order in which he wrote them. At some point he begins numbering them, 8th letter, 13th letter, 17th letter, 33rd letter. At times he gets confused and doubles up on the numbers. There are two 33rd letters. I try to block out the siren song of reading and keep to task. He switches from handwriting to typing once he has an office and a typewriter at his new job at Morris Motors in Oxford. He is now the associate editor of the "Morris Owner Magazine." He writes on lightweight paper, both sides. The sheets are pink, white, or green. Occasionally there is a sentence or two snipped by His Majesty's Examiner, the wartime censor, when Tom verges on content that threatens "the safety of the realm." In one instance he notes the location of a bomb that fell on the outskirts of Oxford. The exact location is excised.

Finally, I achieve my goal. I have laid out the letters on the metal table. There are six piles, 1940, 1941, 1942, 1943, 1944, and 1945, arranged by date in each year. I fold each letter so that the date shows on the upper half, easily visible for future reference. There are 20 letters from the five months immediately following our departure in 1940. There are 30 from 1941, 13 from 1942 and 7 from 1943. In 1944, the numbers dwindle to 5. There is only one saved letter in 1945. There are 76 letters in all.

I read and immerse myself for hours at a time. It doesn't take long before I realize that I can only do a read-through once. Each letter is at least four to six pages, single-spaced, double-sided. I must take nuggets from each as I read. I open a file in Word and name it "Excerpts from THV Letters to Paddy As I Read Through Them." I put a paper clip on each letter when I am finished, like Hansel and Gretel in the forest, marking their trail with pebbles. I want to know where I have been.

CHAPTER 15

1940

~⌒~

I RETURN TO THE FIRST letter. Tom saw us off and came home to Oxford and
7 Lyndworth Close. He writes that Florence and the two grandmas had done
the house, polished the floors, beaten carpets and washed all the clothes. He
has started to paint our room, "the babes" room. (We are always "the babes"
in these letters.) I am struck by all this action, whose purpose is to get the
place ready to rent. But it feels overly efficient and very stiff upper lip. Just
get on with it.

> *I think we can shut up the small bedroom and park our odd stuff in there
> and still get 2.5 (pounds) for the house. With all three bedrooms 2.10.*

Practically speaking, money matters and Tom must move in with his mother
at the far end of the Close. Looking back from this vantage point, however,
it's an uneasy foreshadowing. We never did return.

He writes again a week later. He has rented the house. He gives her a
little war news:

> *Well, I expect you've been hearing we've been having a warm time since
> you left and although so far Oxford hasn't been visited and we've had
> no more alarms, I'm glad with all my heart that I got you and the babes
> away safely when I did.*
>
> *Also what is more important your mother has I think really realised
> now that it was the right thing to do.*

He has an ally in Grandma Dubber as well as his Aunt Gwladys in Lincoln, his father's sister. He and his aunt have been very close since he was a child. Perhaps he welcomes all this support to deflect his own misgivings. However, he recounts in the written memoir of his life that his own mother thought he was crazy to have sent us away. He thinks she ended up by simply feeling sorry for him.

Paddy's long-anticipated cable finally comes, assuring him that she has arrived safely in America. He is thrilled. He believes that she must now be in New York and waits eagerly for her first letter "from the other side." He has already received her letter, written on the train to New York the day after he posted his first to her. Throughout his correspondence, he begins most letters with an accounting of which of her letters he has received and the length of time they took to get to him. There are times when, after news of the sinking of a ship in the Atlantic, he worries that their letters have gone down to the bottom of the sea. Nonetheless, in spite of these happenings and against the backdrop of war, they stay in frequent contact.

In his next letter, August 30th, I am astonished to discover the origins of a famous family story. Never mind Tennessee. We could have gone to India and lived in a palace in Bhopal during the war, courtesy of Auntie Stella's prince, a son of the Nawab and Begum of Bhopal. Aunt Stella was the sister of Ruth Gertrude, my maternal grandmother of Indian origins. She lived in the Bhopal palace and was a sort of nanny to the children. I had heard this tale from my mother over the years but the details were always quite vague.

But no longer. I have it in the original. In the August 30th letter, Tom wrote to Paddy...

First of all you must hear the news from India. Aunt Stella has been very worried (as have all Mummy's relatives out there) by the news, and the slowness and badness of communications these days...Now a few days ago a whole lot of Indian mail arrived all of it posted 2 months ago. One was from Aunt Stella. She said that Mian, one of her princes, had offered off his bat to pay for you and the babes to come out and live in the palace at Bhopal until the end of the war. Just think what you have missed! First

*class passages and money to — well, you know as much as I do about the
sort of life you'd lead. For a short holiday, it'd be marvelous but I think
you'd agree darling that for an indefinite stay it'd be dreadful —and particularly bad for the babes since Mummy assures me that they'd be completely spoilt. Also the trip out would either be quite impossible or very
dangerous, the climate wouldn't do any of you any good and India isn't
my idea of a safe spot anyway. All the same, it's a wonderful thought isn't
it. No one can ever say that you aren't having plenty of chance to travel.*

I take a moment to remind myself of my father's trip, as a three year old,
traveling with his parents on journey from India to England in 1914 at the
outbreak of World War I.

Twists of history, these curious repetitions of experience, are woven
throughout my family history. I can do nothing except to note this. Such
coincidences resist interpretation. I sometimes wonder, though, at the way
in which India became so central to my own life as an adult. So many of
our life-long friendships have their roots in those days. So much so, that we
named our daughter India. A friend of mine, in writing his memoir, speaks
of "memory loops." I can think of no better term to describe the baffling
relationship between past and present. There is no linear trajectory. The
present contains the past. If we are lucky, we can fill in empty spaces, mend
the missing bits in the fabric. As I read my father's letters, I am on my mend-
ing journey.

Tom gets on with life without us. He is involved in war work:

*I have to produce a trained Hotchkiss gun section in a fortnight's time and
while I don't have to do all the lecturing I do have to do all the organizing
and my holiday (starts tomorrow) is looking pretty dog eared already... .*

He has time for pleasant outings:

*I went along the Ridings on Shotover this evening. The weather is keep-
ing clear and bright and today has been gloriously sunny, but there is a*

nip in the mornings. The leaves are beginning to fall and autumn is the season now. There is still some of the heavy summer scent hanging about though…everything is still green and full-blown. I must go up to the Plain one of these evenings and smell the evening when the sun goes in and the earth's pores seem to open. You know the time I mean… .

He takes a holiday with his friend Jacky and family. They go to the historic town of Devizes in Wiltshire. Still there are no air raids in Oxford, but he thinks this will not last. He likes his new job. He will make more money, 455 pounds a year, enough to clear their debt with his mother, Paddy's mother, and Aunt Gwenydd in Lincoln. I am struck by the ordinariness of his life. The war is very much on the periphery. Nothing seems to have changed much except that we are not there.

He looks at the snapshot of Miss Burleson's house which he has received from Miss Everitt, who played a part in selecting Christine as our sponsor.

I have it here as I write and I can just see the babes running about over all that space… .Well my darling keep smiling and enjoy yourself. I've no doubt you'll make the most of your new life and even less that the babes will…I know nothing can make you any different or make you less lovable and I know now piercingly how much I love you.

August becomes September. He has received newspaper clippings of us, photos, as well as an article that appeared in the local newspaper soon after we arrived in Johnson City. He wonders if he can get the originals of the photos, fearing the cuttings will suffer from wear and tear over time. He needn't have worried. Paddy's copies have lasted long enough for me to look at them again today, 73 years later.

In these early letters, my father seems to believe that he has sent his dearly loved ones off on a nice vacation, or perhaps just a short trip. He continually encourages Paddy to enjoy herself and make the most of these opportunities.

Be happy, enjoy yourself, make the most of everything. And the children! I can hardly let myself think of them except to imagine them scampering about the grounds and gardens and being given rides by Rudolph or watching Uncle Jim mow the lawns. Ask them if they remember Tom and their grandmas. Do send me any pictures of them and kiss them and hug them for me and yourself darling, for I want to so much and so often. And remember all the time how much and how much I love you, although I may be a grumpy old bear sometimes. And most of all you needn't worry about coming back to poverty and pinching and scraping after your glorious time out there because you won't have to.

He goes on to tell her that it is her duty to be happy and keep us, the babes, happy. She must not to be worried about anything she may hear or be told about the war raging across the ocean. He will let her know if there is urgent news.

September turns to October. Both Christine and her father, the Dean, find us enchanting. So much so that they suggest that Tom come join us there after the war. Or perhaps it could even be arranged that he could come out now. Tom himself is convinced that he could give us a better life in America but first he must pay off his debts. He allows himself a moment to indulge in this fantasy, Hollywood style:

Oh my sweet, can't you dream somehow what it'll be like when I come stepping off the train? — I can imagine seeing you there with the children and the sun in your hair and the wind holding your dress to all the curves of your body — just like you are in the pictures you have sent.

The war itself still seems not quite real. Oxford remains untouched. At night Tom can see the A.A. barrage over London "like stars bursting all over the sky." In Oxford, he says, less than sixty miles away everything is absolutely peaceful. The war, however, is no fantasy for those who must endure the Luftwaffe's nightly bombing. Paddy's brother, Arthur, and his wife, Mick, come up from London to visit his parents. They have been spending nights in air raid shelters. Once safely in Oxford, they sleep in their pajamas for the first time in six weeks.

By mid October Tom is typing his letters at his office and sending them by air. He gets her letters regularly about two weeks after she posts them. His mood changes. He is letting go of his notion that she is simply vacationing abroad:

> *I don't know where to start. It is just at some times that things feel very bad, and to me bedtime is the worst. It was a wonderful thing for me to be able to come in to you, and know that from that moment nothing else mattered...It is, I think, a very humbling thought that whatever a man may try to do, whatever great work he sets himself to as his life's work, the only really unalterable and everlasting thing in his life will be a single relationship with some other person whom he can only meet by accident, and towards whom he feels emotions over which he can have no possible control...Did you know that the Latin word for children meant "pledges?" I don't think I ever realised quite what that really meant until we got married and had the twins. When shall we see each other again? God knows, darling, but let it be soon, for I ache for you...*

He keeps very busy which help his loneliness. At night he does Home Guard duty and gets as little as two hours of sleep. The Army has given him a very warm overcoat, a steel helmet, a ground sheet, and a haversack. He carries these items everywhere he goes which makes him feel like a "walking Christmas tree." He tells her that he feels much nearer to her when he is writing, "almost as though I am talking to you." He thinks about us children, wondering what we are doing:

> *I wonder what they are saying these days, and even if they remember me now how long they will. When I see them again I'll have to reintroduce myself, won't I... Tell them that Tom loves them.*

As I read, I find occasional hints at what my mother is doing with her life. He is sorry that she misses her encyclopedia. She wants facts about England, such as populations, and the size of the land. He congratulates her for having spoken to a cultural club. Her formal education ended when she was fifteen. In spite of this, she possessed an inquisitive mind and a sharp intelligence. She loved to look things up and encouraged my brother and me to do the same. She gave large Random House dictionaries as Christmas presents. She spent her adult life among very well educated people. She made sure that we had the best education. But she always harbored a sense of her own inadequacy to the point of fearing discovery.

Tom describes a recent trip to London where he must chase a "photographic block" that hasn't arrived. It is needed for the "Morris Owner Magazine," which is about to go to press. He visits his Uncle Walter and Aunt Aileen in Bayswater. He sees the war first hand as he passes through London:

They are living on one of these London squares at No 70. No. 73 had a direct hit about a week ago. There's nothing left of it at all except a mound of broken bricks and glass. 72 and 74 were both cut clean in half, and the current occupants woke up to find their beds hanging out over the street. The people in 70 were all in their shelter when the bomb fell, and nobody was hurt... Another most extraordinary result of bomb damage is what happens (I presume) when a D.A. (delayed action) or perhaps an armour-piercing bomb hits a house. You can look at the house and except for the fact that it looks a bit dilapidated you wouldn't think there was anything wrong with it – until you look at the pavement in front of it. There you will see the edge of a crater which probably extends right under the house which must I suppose be only supported by the next door buildings. The bomb has gone right through the house, and burst after penetrating the earth under its foundations. The result is fantastic – a house without foundations at all.

The letter is heavily censored by His Majesty's Examiner. A block of type is cut out here and there, leaving thin perpendicular strips at each edge, allowing the letter to stay intact.   Even though Oxford is still safe, here is evidence of the dangers we may have escaped. Perhaps Tom feels affirmed in sending us away. It is a good thing, after all, that we are gone. He ends with declarations of his love for her:

> *All my love my darling one, be happy, and remember I love you always and all the time. I really do darling, more I think than I can ever say and certainly much much more than I ever thought I could love anybody at all. Oh, my dearest one I've said this so often, and yet every time it's as if I've thought of something new to tell you about how I'm feeling And when you tell me you love (me) again it's as if I'd never heard it before and a I'm being relieved of a great anxiety because I can never really convince myself that there's any possible reason why someone like you should love someone like me. The other way about yes — for it is only necessary for anyone to know you to love you but you, me. It's just one of those things, I suppose.... Kiss the children hard for me and tell them to save some kisses for me.*

I have certainly invited myself into his life. Am I a welcome guest or should I excuse myself and leave? Am I doing him wrong, exposing his most intimate and passionate self, on display for any eyes to see? What is essential to my story and what is mere voyeurism? He cannot defend himself against my intrusions.

Recently I dreamed that I saw a box of my father's letters on the floor of our church's Parish House. I was concerned that he would see them and know that I was reading them. I asked myself if I should hide them or somehow erase them. The dream ended without giving me an answer. A confession of guilt would receive no absolution.

It is the end of October, 1940. I read that I am budding artist now that I am nearly three years old:

> *Felicity's drawing of grandma was much appreciated. Aunt Gwenydd pointed out that she had given her a nose, two eyes and a mouth, all in*

roughly the right relative positions and that displayed great promise. Also we all loved the message she sent – honestly I think we could all almost hear and see her saying it... .

Tom tells Paddy that as soon as it is possible, he will come to fetch her. But he admits that the war would have to go on for a long time before he could save enough money for that. He is quite sure that he could not take a leave of absence and expect to find his job waiting for him upon his return. "I can't see it happening, that's all." Hopes raised and dashed in two sentences.

He comments on the literature classes Paddy has been taking. He thinks she will find them interesting. He mentions Longfellow, Emerson, Walt Whitman while admitting that he knows very little about the "classical" American writers. We recall that Paddy is living at the home of the Dean of the East Tennessee State Teacher's College. Her sponsor, Christine Burleson, the Dean's daughter, is a teacher and scholar. Paddy seems to have jumped into the academic life feet first. Amazingly, she is getting opportunities for learning that she could scarcely have had back in England.

In this same letter, he makes an interesting suggestion. Unwittingly – and with great naivete - he seems to be giving her permission to roam:

And my darling one, if it wasn't likely to make me so jealous I really do wish and hope (with part of me) that you could find someone for a friend, or someone to take some small part of my place, and yet I don't because it makes me so proud and happy to know that I mean so much to you...I don't own you – I hate the thought of possessive love, but we're a man and a woman and it's there in the background all the time.

Does he want to relieve himself of her somehow? Is he thinking, I have sent you away and I feel bad about it, so please do go out and have a good time? He also seems to be asking permission for himself to do the same.

Again I feel like an intruder. These two people, my parents, are struggling to redefine who they are in relation to each other now that they are separated by war and thousands of miles of sea. I tell myself that I am simply curious about how they will manage. I reassure myself that I am not a voyeur. And I keep on reading.

By mid November, 1940, Tom is looking ahead to Christmas and sends a package off to us. He writes that it contains a darts board, some tweed dress material, and little books for our birthday on December 12th. He labels the package "CHRISTMAS PARCEL FOR ENGLISH REFUGEES." A new rule allows refugees to receive packages duty free. So now we are "refugees," no longer simply "evacuees." Are we lumped into the "huddled masses yearning to be free", people seeking refuge in America never to return? Reading this letter now, the perspective shifts, a tiny kaleidoscopic rearrangement. It foreshadows what is yet to come.

Tom, however, is still living in a future of his own devising. He has a glorious vision:

> *I can see you now my darling with the light on your face as you looked towards the white wall of Christine's house through your window as you wrote to me the other week; I can hear the high-pitched voices and the patter of the children's feet as they rampage about the garage. I can see the wind blowing your dress about the curves of your body (darling I thought you wanted to get plump again!) and I can see Peter tearing along with his dark hair flying out and Felicity champing along behind him with her fat knees rubbing together. Darling, you are the most beautiful loving thing in the world for me and the children are as beautiful and lovable as you are, and as perfect, because they came from you. Be happy, and wait for me my own dearest one for I shall surely come and take you again, and it'll be as if we were knowing one another for the first time all over again.*

He isn't the only one who has fantasies of the future. Christine offers to give him a farm in Florida. He expresses his gratitude to her while also acknowledging that he is not a farmer. He says he has a lot of gumption, however, "which is what it takes."

There are now hints coming from Paddy that she may not be fully enjoying her trip away from England. He encourages her to be honest with him and tell him what's going on. He takes this opportunity to reassert the rightness of his decision to send us away:

There is one thing that as I have said already is quite certain and that is at no time since you went have I been in any doubt as to whether I was right in sending you. In fact I don't think I have ever thought that I could have done anything different which is why I find it rather difficult to answer people who say 'I don't know how you could part with them.' There are still 100,000 children in London which shows you that my attitude isn't general.

He goes on to clarify his position in strong political terms. He is, of course, concerned about food shortages and the possibility of physical danger; but these are not at the top of the list:

Also even if it were not for food shortage and bombs I would not have stay (sic) in England for the other reason which I have very good cause to remember myself from the time of the last war — I mean the poisoning and starving of their minds. They would grow up at the best in an atmosphere of hate and flase (sic) religion and sentimentality — they are praying at the children in the BBC Children's hour now, telling them pray for their brothers and daddies fighting against evil and wicked men! Of course they needn't listen to the childrens' hour if they don't want to, but much the same sort of thing is happening or will soon be happening in all the schools — there was a case reported in the papers the other day of a schoolteacher getting into hot water for allowing his pupils to sing "The Watch on the Rhine." Straws at the moment but the wind is beginning to flow all right. I don't suppose I really got it out of my head that the Germans were some sort of ogres until I went to Germany and found out my mistake and that was when I was twenty! The hate propaganda on the children will be much more intensive this time too because the war is so much nearer home. Thank God they're away from that and won't have to spend all the years unlearning what I had to.

It is hard to know what to do with this. Were we sent away to preserve our minds? What is he not seeing? The Luftwaffe is pounding London, Coventry, and Birmingham every night. France has fallen and Paris is entertaining the Gestapo. On the other hand, he attempts to justify the loss of his wife and children through some notion that we need to be able to speak kindly of the German people. One cannot fault his generosity and good will. He never could have conceived of the horror and cruelty to come. That was beyond human imagining. Perhaps he should be pitied, instead, for the price being exacted by his political passions.

But it didn't work. Some years ago, while we were living in Washington, my husband and I went to the movies to see "Schindler's List." When we left the theater, to say that I was angry would be too easy. I was enraged. At that moment, it was utterly clear to me that it was the Germans who had driven me away from my first home, my extended family, and my father. This is the truth of my life. That my life has turned out well does not change this fact. I was astonished at the strength of my reaction. I had absorbed the hatred that he sought to spare us. I am a singer. I love to sing Italian. I can do French and Spanish reasonably well, too, but my first teacher could never get me to sing German. I told her I just can't do it. I found the language ugly, in spite of the loveliness of the music.

Tom is now writing at the end of December, 1940. We became three years old on the twelfth of the month. We have had our first American Christmas. Paddy will be 27 on the fifth of January. He sends her birthday wishes:

You have no age, for you are youth itself. You will never grow old as people understand growing old because it just isn't in you. From your pictures you look to me as youthful and fresh as you did when I first saw you but you have gained in poise and a certain property of repose and quietness which you always had in you but which you did not use to allow full play...Whenever we have a lovely night as we did last night with a great glimmering moon and quiet mists about the flanks of the hills I think how we could appreciate it, we two together. And I think too of the pleasure we shall have in watching our children growing up in the

*same way, learning to be happy and being happy themselves making oth-
ers happy. I see no other object in life. How Peter and Felicity will set
about it I don't know. Maybe they will be geniuses more likely they will
be ordinary half and half people like me.*

I try to imagine how she would experience his fulsome praise. There she is,
among strangers and forced to attune her life to theirs, with little opportunity
to act independently. Does she welcome his love and caring and gain strength
from it? Or does she gradually see him as hopelessly out of touch with her
situation? He helps me with an answer:

*First of all I know how you feel about your present life. It's beastly hav-
ing to live with people in the way you are having to – that is without any
choice, and dependent on their good will; and besides having your best
friends taken away from you as soon as you were getting to know them…
My dearest one I read all the things you said about me and it made me feel
happy and ashamed and proud all at once for I know that of the combination you are the sun and I am the moon if I am anything at all. I have no
strength and no power but what you have given me, and that is the thing
that I feel perhaps most unnatural about your present life – that you have
not the opportunity of giving. In scientific terms you are an extrovert –
your character and your creative impulses are all turned outwards away
from yourself – you fulfill yourself through other people. Your organizing
ability is a sign of that.*

He knows her well. He would also recognize me. People fuel me, give me
energy and pleasure.

CHAPTER 16

1941

THE YEAR TURNS. IT IS January, 1941, five months into our new life. We have returned from our driving trip to Florida with Christine and Mrs. Devine. Tom lavishes praise on Paddy's written narrative of that journey. He writes of her simple and effective ability to evoke powerful images of what she has seen. He says he enjoyed every word of it. He can envision us, for he is our father and we are his children:

> *So Peter calls them "pecalums," I've never seen one in my life, except maybe at the Zoo... . I'm rather surprised Peter wasn't so keen on paddling as Felicity; and yet perhaps not. Obviously he would be keen on making sand castles. Like most girls (as compared with most boys) she would tend to live more for the moment and to prefer sensual pleasures to creative ones – to get pleasure out of her surroundings as they are and to see beauty in what she sees, instead of trying to make things as she wants them to be (the male way). Gosh I wish I could see them now; they must be fascinating. Never mind, darling, there's plenty of time, yet, and the best years of a child's life are between two and twelve – I've got another nine years before they start growing away from us.*

Rather innocently, he stuffs us into our little gender boxes. But what else does he know? He is new to fatherhood and leans on his preconceptions. Distance and war make it difficult for him to do otherwise.

By February it is clear that there is trouble on Roan Hill. Paddy and Christine are not getting along. Tom receives a letter from Christine laying it all out. She cites Paddy's "hunger for the momentary sensation." She states that her and her father's "bookish reverence for the past and our efforts toward future accomplishments" are meaningless to Paddy. Christine spills her anger all over the page. Paddy has "a perfect right to be herself at all costs, but we cannot allow ourselves to be annihilated in the process." She claims that the schedule she and her father have been forced to maintain over the past four months has worn down her energy. She cannot continue in this way. She and her father will give Paddy $75 a month for living expenses when she moves out. In Christine's mind, this is already a done deal. She softens a bit at the end and gives us, the children, a free pass. "In the narrower personal sense, the babies ahve wort itvery [sic] decidedly." The scholar in her takes a back seat to her rage. Her typing falls apart.

Tom finds himself caught between these two utterly incompatible women. He replies to Christine:

Dear Christine,

I was very sorry indeed to get your letter. I must say that I was surprised also, as I have heard nothing from Paddy but the warmest appreciation of your kindness to her and to the twins. Although it was obvious to me from the first that you and she were of widely differing types and tastes, there has been no suggestion of such complete incompatibility as you describe, and I hope you will believe me when I say that she has repeatedly shown in her letters to me — not by fulsome praise, but in words which I can understand better than most people — that she is really and deeply grateful for all that you have done for us....

It is not that he does not believe her nor is he laying blame. Simply put, Christine and Paddy are a really bad fit. He writes of the difficulty of being on the receiving end of help;

The practical proof of gratitude is so difficult with some people, particularly enforced gratitude to someone who was less than six months ago entirely unknown. Paddy is an active "doing" sort of person, and she has little opportunity now to act, think, or do things for herself at all. Remember she had a home to organize and look after, she had me, she had our own circle of friends over here. All these she has lost, and although it may seem an unfeeling thing to say, I know you will understand me when I say that no amount of kindness and generosity can make up for them.

He could not have said it more clearly. He is an intelligent, sensitive, and caring young man with a gift for expressing himself on the written page.

Upon receiving Christine's letter, he writes to Paddy:

My darling,

Let's get the unpleasant part over first. I am enclosing a copy of a letter I received from Christine last week and a copy of my reply. I don't know whether she told you she was writing to me but I rather assumed that she didn't. In any case it would probably better if you didn't let her know that you have seen them.

There is, of course a lot to be said that I haven't said to her. First, I was not entirely surprised – although the letter was a bit of a shock – because in spite of her generosity she seems to have been behaving in a very unreasonable manner in some directions....I must say I was a bit upset when I read the letter, and took it at rather more than face value. However, the next day I received yours which was posted on the same day which made no reference to any specific bust-up but included the very illuminating remark that you were under the impression that Christine disliked you so much that she could hardly bring herself to speak to you. Under such circumstances the whole letter can obviously be read in a very different light.

Christine, he believes, is jealous. Unlike Paddy, who has children, good looks, and charm, she has only her father and her books:

The way of helping others she conceives to be the best is this extraordinary American system of spreading gobbets of culture about wholesale. The "bookish reverence for the past" she refers to is partly this ingrained preference and partly a form of escape from life. She has apparently never got down and found out what people really think — I mean the people she is out to do good to — her whole approach to the question of living is an artificial and literary one. So when a large vital piece of real life, like you and the twins comes barging into her scheme of things she doesn't like it at all. And tries to get back into her shell.

Tom was extraordinarily prescient. In 1967, at the age of 68, Christine shot herself. The first shot didn't kill her, but the second one did. Back in her shell for good. I learned this while trolling the Internet. I found reference to a play that had been written about her life and especially about her death. The playwright set out to examine the time between the two shots. I also found a Shakespearean scholar who knew her work. We exchanged a couple of emails. He sent me photos of the house where she had taken her life. He assumed I would recognize it and referred to us as the "orphans" she had taken in during the war. The house, a far cry from Roan Hill, was a rough looking cabin in a state of disrepair. He suggested that her academic career had not succeeded as she had wished. She had become isolated and without a future she could envision.

In this account history seems to have made us motherless. How did Christine tell our story after we left? Did she eliminate Paddy from her narrative totally while preserving us, the children, as evidence of her own generosity and good will?

Perhaps she wanted people to remember that she had done her bit for England during the war. But she had no place for Paddy. Conveniently she seems to have turned us into orphans. What better way to kill two birds with one stone? The first bird is Paddy, whom she wanted to get rid of with a parting gift of $75 a month. The second bird would have been her own culpability in the affair. No mother, no problem. Just Christine taking two lost children into her heart. We shall never know the truth of the matter, but

I get a certain pleasure from these speculations. There is no one to counter my imaginings. In the end, these are all stories. Now I am the storyteller and can do as I wish. I do not have to imagine Tom's story, however. He tells it on every thin, aging and faded page.

On March 18, 1941, he writes that he is glad things are so much easier for Paddy now. Apparently, we are not being thrown out after all. He tells her that he has written to Christine:

> *As far as Christine is concerned, I have done all I can do, and I have told her so with the proviso that she can always treat me as a safety valve if she wants to. I think she will in the end be able to get something out of her relationship with you, but only if she stops trying to compare you with her ideas of what she thought you were going to be. She certainly has much more than the average sense and sensibility, and if she lets the former have a chance against the latter, she will be a lot happier and in the end a lot better off.*

He is characteristically honest with Paddy as he shares the letter that Christine has written to him:

> *I think you hurt her pretty badly when you told her about her jealousy, and so on: you have a knack of letting rip with really damaging home truths when you are roused as everyone who knows you knows. She admits that she can find nothing to like in you and she's mad as hell because she can't get it inside — all the same is a cultured and reasonable person and knows that she shouldn't be, and that has produced a real psychological jam.*

The "home truths" hit home with me. I have often thought, and at times, said to others, that I am very nice until I am not. And when I am not, my heat rises and I speak out. I like to believe that I target issues of social justice, particularly where I perceive unfairness and victimization of the innocent. But I also know that at times I can be damaging and personal. I am no stranger to making apologies. And in this I differ from Paddy. She did not soften her little cruelties by saying she was sorry.   Christine seems to approach an apology when she writes, "we both expected the wrong thing: she, the care-free American family she had heard about, and I one of my old friends from L.M.H. " [Lady Margaret Hall, her Oxford college.]   She and Paddy move on from here and we stay on Roan Hill.

Tom and Paddy's dialogue continues.   I am listening but have only his voice in my ears.   Hers is faint, second hand and filtered through him.   They hit a little bump in the road, a misunderstanding.   He writes:

My dearest one, when shall I see you again? Oh, I know it's selfish of me to say such things – I ought to concentrate on the 99% of my time when I am getting on perfectly happily with my daily jobs, and the 1% when I think of you with such absolutely terrible longing. I can't help it. And then most of the time I can recognize how incredibly lucky I am – no need to worry about you or the children, in a safe, easy job, in an unblitzed area – but just occasionally I feel almost savagely that I would prefer all those worries just so long as I had you by my side. That shows you how selfish these thoughts are, because I know that in my worst moments I couldn't think of exposing you and the children to the dangers both poten-tial and real of life in war-time England. If I could only see some sense in it – if I could only believe that this war is really being fought for something worth fighting for – it wouldn't be so bad. But in these moments I can only see that in owing to the corrupt and evil way in which the countries of the world are governed I have been robbed of the only thing that makes life worth living, and the other compensations just aren't worth having.

He has made a bit of a mess of things, reducing her to taking up a mere 1% of his time.   His political banner is flying high in back drop.   He sees himself at the mercy of the global ravages of corrupt governments.

She doesn't like what he says.   We hear her voice in his reply.   He tries to explain himself.   He apologizes for writing "a lot of conceited nonsense."   He upset her and he is sorry.   Perhaps he was trying to persuade himself that he wasn't lonely at all.

We cannot know if she was comforted by this. Perhaps on her side she has been trying to spare him her discontent. Would she rather be in England? Most likely. He responds rather sharply to something she has said:

> *There is one thing I must clear up; I'm not leading a "full life" no one over here is. It is impossible to live a "full" life under the constant threat if (sic) something – I don't know what, or quite how to put it: everything that is done is either directly connection with the war or conditioned by it, and that makes the whole thing like a nightmare if you allow yourself to think about it....Believe me darling there's nothing fine or noble or satisfying in it at all. The point is darling that you needn't think you are missing anything by being out of it: I won't say your presence would make me feel better about the whole bloody business, because it wouldn't. The one thing that I am glad about is that you and the children are away from it all; but it would help me to forget it sometimes.*

He is still sure he is right to have sent us away. A cross-Channel invasion seems a certainty. He cautions her about trying to come home. He fears the war will be fought out on British soil.

It is March. We have been gone since August. He still believes in a future that will include us. He writes to her on his birthday, May 8, 1941. He turns 30.

> *Today is my birthday and I have left the sunny twenties for good and all – isn't it odd? In ten years I shall be forty – and that seems a damned sight odder. And ten years time the children will be thirteen, and you will be thirty seven, and we'll be happy comfortable and settled – and pleased to goodness aware of what is going on around us, able to enjoy the good things of life with the fullest appetite.*

I feel a great sadness. It never happened this way. He could not have conceived that we are gone forever. When did I stop imagining him? Throughout my life, he was never even a memory. At the time, I was too young to articulate my loss. But as I read his words and write my own, I know that loss is stored somewhere inside me. Over the years, I have brushed up against it. A tiny core of depression lies at the center of my otherwise active and fairly vibrant self, a flowering of anxiety before even the simplest trip, particularly those by plane. An obsessive need to clean the house and pay the bills before I leave.

Many years ago I was travelling to a business conference with three young men, my colleagues, two were psychologists and one a social worker. We were flying and I had warned them that I didn't do well on planes. Among themselves they assigned me a "minder" for the flight. Richard, not content merely to sit next to me, wondered and asked, "Felicity, what are you afraid of?" Instantly, without a moment's thought, I said, "That I can't get back." Ever the clinician, he had tweaked my unconscious. I was amazed. I began to understand the roots of my fear.

Now I am going back, a time traveler on my father's letters. I am grateful. Grateful to him for writing them, grateful to my mother for carrying them through our wartime odyssey, for storing them for decades curiously out of sight and out of mind. Did she really forget she had them? Again I wonder why she made no mention of their existence. For now, I suspect no deep reason, just her need to get on with things, move forward, bury the past.

I return to Tom's story. In the midst of trials with Christine, his own loneliness, and the pointlessness of the war, he still has his children very much in his mind. He relishes every little piece of news of our doings. He takes joy in our accomplishments and envisions our growth:

I thought their drawings were marvelous, especially Felicity's mouse. I would hardly have believed it possible that children of their age could have produced such work. I mean there is real observation and an ability to transfer three-dimensional things into two dimensions, which is really an acquired knack you wouldn't think they were old enough to be able to grasp. Peter's fish and his boy at the end of the kite string were good too – you can see the different technique – obviously Felicity is much more painstaking while Peter is all for the broad effects and apt to be slapdash. Are they going to be artists I wonder?

Did our mother ask us to draw picture for our father? Did we have any idea who he was? I have always believed that he was completely lost to us once we arrived in America. But not so after all. I am drawing pictures for him.

He sees a film of us that she has sent:

> *Do you remember what little skinned rabbits they were when they were born and now just to think of them! One of the things that struck me more than anything about it at a second showing – and it struck Bernard too – is the fact that the children have stopped "toddling" – particularly Peter. They walked in a singing, free confident way, and though its' myself that says it, very gracefully. Peter seems to be still physically almost fearless and does everything with complete self abandonment and confidence; particularly I noticed that when they were bending down to the goldfish pond: Peter just goes straight down, while Felicity was much more careful and doing the job gradually in two or three stages.*

He asks when he can expect our first letters, saying that he has such a high opinion of us that we will be able to write at least two years before other children of our age. He feels that he knows us and he does in a way. We may not have been writing at the age of three, but we are writers. For me, it is something I have done throughout my life in whatever way I can--be it a casual travel journal, a letter, or a published professional article. My brother made his career as a writer, a journalist whose beat spanned everything from sports to arts criticism.

Tom even gets a chance to participate in one of our childhood dramas, the frightening fall of one of us into the fish pond:

> *I was thrilled to hear about Peter's feat. Was the fish-pond deep enough to be out of Felicity's depth. Because if it was he must have saved her life! Honestly darling it's wonderful to know they are so sensible, and able to look after themselves – and I shouldn't think they'll ever go too near the water again without taking proper care. Tell Peter I am very proud of him, and that he must always look after his sister like that: and tell*

Felicity how Tom is glad to hear that she got wet and spoilt her dungarees, and how glad he is that she is safe and sound and how clever she must have been not to lose her head and to get out of the pond with Peter's help.

He has received "snaps" of us:

Quite suddenly our children have grown up and for my memory of two fat, chubby little toddlers — certainly no babies, but directly recognizable as the babies they had been — I have to substitute all of a sudden a little boy and a little girl of a loveliness that made my inside turn right over when I saw. My darling, Felicity has turned into the most perfect thing I ever saw; and like you with her smile and her awareness and the open joy of her expression. They look, especially Felicity, more like five than three years old. I suppose I ought to have been forewarned by your descriptions of them…but all your accounts left me unprepared for what they have actually turned into. Such lovely firm graceful bodies are rare enough but with all that is in their faces and their attitudes and much more what is promised there as well.

He is proud and humble, feeling himself unbelievably lucky to be "mixed up so intimately with people I would ordinarily be quite content to admire at a distance." He fears he risks becoming conceited.

Though still physically distant from Oxford, the war makes a dramatic appearance. Tom is standing outside his office building, "out at the back of the Works" with one of his machine gunners whom he trains. The man suddenly looks up and says, " Look. Hasn't that chap got four engines?"

I turned round and there sure enough, quite low and coming towards us was a big bomber with four engines. That may not seem odd to you out there but the four-engined machine is still a bit of a rarity in these parts.

The plane approaches them at a great speed. High above it they see fighters, Spitfires and Hurricanes "in a hurry too but they didn't seem to be gaining on it to any extent." Tom and his companions are puzzled. They know planes. They work for a company, Morris Motors (the "Works") that builds them. Perhaps it is a British Stirling or a Halifax. However, those are still semi-secret with no published pictures available yet:

> *We had to rely on our own knowledge of the characteristics of the builders and on the usual "experts" who are always on hand at times like these. We decided it was a Stirling, and admired it out of sight. Before it had disappeared, someone said "Look, there's another! And along she came following the first, and again very low, and more high-flying escorting fighters. This time there was no doubt as to what she was. "Yank," said one. "One of those Consolidateds." It was a Liberator – I don't know the American designation – and she looked as big and fast as the Stirling.*

They are seeing their first American made B-24 bomber, as well as the new British Stirling:

> *But that was only the beginning! No fewer than eight of these mammoths flew by and from the direction they were coming from and the screens of fighters who droned by high overhead the whole time, I should imagine they were returning from a 'business' trip over Germany or occupied France. It was a sight I won't forget for a long time.*

I have read and reread this passage. Each time I get a thrill. I see a few men, out for a smoke, taking a break. Suddenly the sky fills. They call to others to come out. I hear their excited voices, see their upraised hands, pointing as these great new machines appear. I can almost hear the roar of engines.

Tom types this letter on May 5, 1941, his 44th letter. He adds a handwritten postscript, crammed into the last available space at the bottom of the final page. "According to this morning's papers, America is now 'in' the war. I must say I didn't gather that from FDR's speech; but then 'politician-ese' isn't a language I understand very well."

But he does understand what he has seen in the skies above Oxford that day. Does his reach extend to question his certainty that we will be reunited, that we will live out our lives together as a family? Not so far, anyway, for he promises to take Paddy to New York when he comes to America. In New York he says, "we will have a real bust, something that will repay all your poverty and the long, long time of absence. I'll leave all the arrangements to you!"

He goes up to London on business by train. A blast of steam from a nearby engine brings us back to him, if only for a moment:

On the way back we stopped in a station just opposite of an engine which was off the other way. Shortly before it went it started blowing off steam and I thought ever so vividly of how we stood on the platform at Euston, you holding Felicity, and me Peter, waiting for the boat train to come in, and how an engine just the other side suddenly started blowing off steam and how Peter jumped in my arms, but didn't cry, just looked very wide-eyed, frightened rather but interested at the time but Felicity cried like anything. How long ago that seems now, and yet only yesterday when I think of our last embrace and how I stood on the end of the platform, and at the last minutes you got to the window and waved to me and how I watched you out of sight.

This is me crying. Out of sight for nineteen years.

But I am a singing child, not really so very unhappy. Tom loves to hear the stories Paddy tells. He finds them delightful:

Especially the one about Felicity singing in Sunday School! I can just picture her doing it because one of my most vivid memories is of her 'dancing' in the middle of the room, just going round in circles and wagging her head.

And I think too of Peter hanging out of the pram and sticking twigs in the wheels, and Felicity shouting "Back 'ome!" and roaring with laughter.

I am delighted with these stories, too. I had a life before August, 1940. I had a father and he remembers me. He tells me who I was then. I recognize this child. She is very much like me. I am still singing in church, though I have graduated from Sunday School.

Tom sees us on films that Paddy sends:

They were so lovely and brought home to me so sharply all the things about you and the children that I am missing that I really felt quite bad for a moment or two – and it's damned selfish of me to feel that way – and even more to let onto you that I did – but I can't help it…there were certain things that stuck- Peter and Felicity in their nighties outside the house climbing about and being so smug about it, and you tickling Peter's feet on the sandpile and all the lovely crimson clover and Felicity still tending to waddle but Peter running about with such grace and speed, and your hair – oh darling how lovely it is so soft and silk and how it flows about and how much better it is than anyone else's I have ever seen.

By July 1941, Paddy's discontent with her situation on Roan Hill re-emerges. Paddy wants to come home. But it will take more than a pram ride to get her there.

It is awfully enticing to think of your coming over here again, but on the whole darling I don't think so. I could always raise enough money on the house to pay for your passage, but then where would we live? And what would happen to the children? They mustn't come back whatever you do, and I can't see Christine would be able to look after them nor would it be right to ask her to.

I find this unnerving. Had she really thought she could leave us behind? A month later he responds, sympathetic and hopeful.

I can imagine how you must feel sometimes – it is hideous having to live with people with whom you can't establish any real contact. From all you say it appears as if the worst is over as far as Christine is concerned and that you have both managed to establish a sort of basis to get on together with…the feeling of being a sort of ornament about the place must be absolute hell at times

He is in for a shock. Scarcely two weeks pass before he receives her 44th letter, dated August 22nd. He writes back:

I certainly had no idea that things had got to quite a pitch of definiteness, and that Christine had actually give you marching orders….I take it however that the main trouble is the old incompatibility between the two of you, the old jealousy and possessiveness on her part. She wants the twins but she doesn't want you — is that it? You say the best way of dealing with that particular form of selfishness is to take them away as well. But it does seem pretty difficult. As for the other plan, honestly darling when I knew that you actually almost got to the pitch of doing it, I came over so weak and full of delicious and agonizing feelings that I knew at once that I would be quite incapable of offering reliable advice.

Is our mother seriously considering leaving us and fleeing back to Tom? How shall he respond? He delays his reply as he "threshes the thing over" in his mind. Finally he writes on September 9th.:

The only definite conclusion I can come to is this, and it's not very helpful I'm afraid. You'll have to decide for yourself whether the children will be all right if you leave them with Christine;

As he continues, he betrays an appalling lack of understanding of what children need:

After all, for a year or two yet they don't want anything except plenty of food fresh air and somewhere to play. I don't want them to grow up into American small town snobs, but there's no danger of that development

95

taking place for a considerable time ahead. And I would say (and this is purely selfish — how could I think it otherwise?) that if you're going to leave them at all, you should come to me.

He is his own battleground:

That's how I feel — it's not the way I think because I know it is wrong and that there are a thousand good reasons why I should keep you out in U.S.A. and a single one why I should bring you home away from the children, to a hard and fairly uncomfortable and probably dangerous life in England — and all the more so since I may be called up and then we shouldn't have anymore chance of being together than we have now. But that is a risk which you must decide for yourself is worth taking or not — at best it would mean that we should be together but away from the children, possibly for years, at worst that I should be not a great deal worse off than I am now (emotionally I mean — a great worse off financially) while you would have lost the children and got nothing in return except your own country and a few of your friends. I have so little to lose that I can't make a decision with any honesty.

He sums it up and abandons the field to her:

Put it this way; theoretically either course can be justified; you should stay with the children not because it's your duty or anything like but because you are the right person to bring them up — and I don't care how efficient or otherwise Christine may be. Alternatively you should come home because the crucial point in their lives when they will really need intelligent handling won't arrive for sometime yet. Oh, God, I'm going round in circles.

She seems to have already arrived at her own conclusions. He acknowledges this, though we cannot know what she said:

On the whole though I think you have taken the right decision, and I won't try to dissuade you from it however much I may want to. Whether the children will be well looked after or not, one of us should be at least within call in case anything happens and so your place is I think in the U.S.A. – if not with them then somewhere about where you can at least see them sometimes.

I am shocked by all this. It is hard to believe that she would have left us behind. Of course, she didn't. But I wonder at her state of mind that she would even consider it. She longs for home, and Tom longs for her. But there we are, the children, standing between them. He says that he can see clearly now that she must not come back and that he has no right to ask her to. He says again that he never regrets having sent us away.

He begins his very next letter with wonderful news that he may be getting a new job. He will now be an "Outside Chaser" for Morris. He will travel the country to subcontractors responsible for aircraft manufacturing, "keeping them up to scratch with their deliveries, and if they aren't, finding out why." He is thrilled. He feels he will be useful now in the war effort.

He returns to her. He wonders if she is still at Roan Hill. He returns to his own home, half expecting to find her there. She fills his dreams. In spite of his longing, he is beginning to build up another life, in compensation for what he has lost. He knows he must do things as differently as possible from what they used to do together.

He understands himself well. He is deliberate in choosing his new life. He wraps himself in metaphorical clothing and finds comfort:

Our life together is like a nice coat I took off when you went away. When I'm out wearing another coat, I don't think about it much, but when I open the wardrobe in the evenings there it is hanging up just to remind me. And of course I often open the wardrobe for no reason at all except just to look at it.

On her end, Paddy has made her move:

Your letter dated the 2ⁿᵈ of September arrived on Saturday with the great
news that you have made your escape and are on your own again.

What grand news darling. The new house sounds absolutely perfect —
and I know you are a good judge of such things so that it makes me want
more than ever to share it with you. Perhaps some day I shall.

What house? Where? I don't know. Perhaps we are in the little gatehouse
now, no longer in the main house. At any rate, Christine is still supporting us
with $100 a month. Tom reviews Paddy's financial situation with her. Will
she be able to manage? How will she find housekeeping in America? Will she
find a "coloured" woman to help? Are there any white servants in her part of
the world? He is quite satisfied with the outcome with regard to Christine.

In October a new actor, waiting in the wings comes on stage. He is Lynn,
the son of the English family who live across the road. Tom is nervous:

How much does Lynn mean to you? I am jealous of him, quite naturally, and
I am probably right in saying it without reason. I would just like to know.
And if he has helped your happiness in any way he is my friend. That's all.

Tom has run into Lynn before and doesn't think very much of him. In
his view Lynn is uneducated and ignorant of the world beyond the hills of
Tennessee. Tom has even gone so far as to say that he has the makings of "an
embryo storm trooper." However, he tries to be kind:

Lynn is a queer lad but from all you have told me a real good one — as
you don't need telling you have to take people as you find them and his
possessiveness is at least a fault on the right side. But don't go falling in
love with him will you darling?

He takes time out of his personal worries to reflect on the war. He wonders about current feelings among Americans. Unnervingly, he sees into the
future:

I expect they're more worried about the Japs who are making lots of nasty faces just now; on reason alone I can't believe that they would be mad enough to take on the Eastern Red Army (who have already given them two damned good hidings), the Chinese (who've just given them a third) and the Americans as well. Perhaps they reckon that the USA would 'non-intervene' in an attack on Siberia. But imperialist expansion is an unreasonable thing and may make the Japs commit suicide in this way. And to give them their due it is my opinion (backed by an eminent naval authority Lt. P.L. Vaughan) [his brother] that the Japanese navy can blow the U.S. Pacific fleet out of the water — See what your friends say about that!

November comes and goes. Her letters are growing more infrequent. On December 7, 1941, he writes, as yet unaware that the U.S. Pacific Fleet has indeed been blown out of the water at Pearl Harbor. Finally, America is at war. There will be no cross-Atlantic travels for Tom or Paddy. She will not be arranging trips to New York for them. There will be no farm in Florida, no Hollywood-style embrace when he steps off a train. Nor will she turn up unexpectedly on his doorstep. His fantasy will die. The world has turned.

He brings up the Lynn again. This relationship will change the game as well for some time to come. Paddy has clearly become more deeply involved. Tom cautions her:

The question of you and Lynn. From what you say it sounds to me as though you are much more in control than you think you are. As for getting hurt you know as well as I do that it's impossible to go through life and have real relationships with people without hurting and getting hurt. It's how you take it.

He concocts a rather strange brew of politics, religion, and pugilism as he attempts to explain himself:

As for comparisons between my way of looking at things and Lynn's it isn't worth making them unless you can draw the correct conclusions from them. The only conclusions I can get from it which seems to make any sense is that the capitalist system with its biased education and lying religions has made Lynn incapable of using his brains and me of using my fists. As for the contrasts you draw – breeding, pride and so on – they're nothing. I'm a product of my environment and he of his. Good and bad don't come into it. It's just the way things are. My personal opinion is that he is a better man than I am, and you can tell him that from me. Nonetheless I mean to keep hold of you forever and beyond, if necessary, and if it looks like coming to the pinch I shall take boxing lessons. I'm not joking! Tell him I weigh 12-2. [12 stone 2 pounds is about 170 pounds].

It is not clear why Lynn, in Tom's perspective, is a "better man," unless he might be better with his fists, a most manly thing.

A week later, Tom writes that he learned news of the attack on Pearl Harbor just after posting his last letter. The time for idle speculation and loving chatter is over. He is now very concerned that prices will rise, making it increasingly difficult for Christine to support us. He takes on Lynn with a new sense of urgency. He lays down conditions. He is not so nice anymore:

(i) *I am not going to give you any easy way out. If it ever comes the pitch of choosing between me and Lynn you will have to do it in the open and when I have had a chance of being seen by you again.*

(ii) *I shall want the children. This is a very difficult thing for me to say because it sounds on the face of it like hurting you wantonly. The fact is I could not be content with their being brought up by Lynn and in the sort of atmosphere he and his circles move in. This is in no sense a denunciation since what he is, he is; but I want Peter and Felicity to be balanced, responsible citizens of the world and to be given as far as possible a true scale of values to build their lives on. I can hardly see them getting that in the American middle classes who I have come to the conclusion are all a bit crazy in one direction or another. You with me or you by yourself (probably better) could give them that but not you with Lynn. Alternatively if anything happens to me then I am in strong favour of your keeping them, as against your or my mother. Looking back, that's a rather silly thing to say because there will then be no problems left but you might want to know what I think about it.*

He fears she is drifting without thought. He is trying to rescue her from herself and a feared unhappy outcome. He will want us, though he hasn't yet figured out how he would actually get us. From 3,000 miles distance in the middle of a war he asserts his rights as a father. One could say it is a little late for that, considering how eager he was to send us away. Life in America has now become toxic to our development whereas not so long ago he saw it as a haven where our minds would be free from the poison of anti-German propaganda. It is all quite a muddle. He backs off and tries to reassure her of his love.

I have travelled on my father's letters for a year and several months. My journey began in August 1940. I have arrived, as if by train, at December, 1941. This is his last letter of the year, a way station written two days after my brother's and my fourth birthday. We pass into 1942 without champagne and confetti.

CHAPTER 17

1942

I NEED TO STOP HERE for a moment, take a breath, and look around me. My father is here beside me as I travel. I am hitchhiking on his words as I create memories for myself. The empty spaces within me fill as I write. Now I can talk to others about him as if I really knew him then. After we left, I say, my father lived with his mother in Oxford and worked for Morris Motors. He joined the Home Guard and stayed up at night to watch for enemy aircraft. He travelled to London on business and saw blitzed ruins. He missed us very much and may have wished that he hadn't sent us away.

I read more letters. I fear he is seeing through me:

And I must say speaking professionally, that writing is an art. And every art is about 5% talent or inclination or inspiration or what you will and 95% damned hard work. A man who "leaves someone else to finish off his stuff" is just another lazy bugger after some easy money. He isn't a writer and won't be if he does it for the rest of his life.

Of course, his admonitions are not directed at me. But I take them to heart. He accompanies me as I go down to the kitchen for chocolate and tea. Get back upstairs to your office. Nothing will get done unless you do it. There will be no words to darken this page unless you write them.

So I persevere. Here is his first letter of the year, written on January 7th, 1942. Peter and I have had our tonsils out. He is shocked at the cost and worries about our fright. Even this he turns into a political issue:

It frightens me too as I realize how much I stand to lose by having passed my responsibilities over to a people and a system I have never trusted.

Increasingly I see his ideological self, that part of him firmly wedded to notions of a Utopian society lived in a Communist world, a world now threatened by Fascism. I let it go for now. But the subtext is always there, the lens through which he views the war, the future, and all that is good and right.

He returns to Lynn, who is becoming more than just a thorn in his side. He learns that Lynn, who is in the Navy, is going away. What is there to say, except that perhaps it will give Paddy a chance to find out how she really feels about him.

As far as Tom is concerned, Lynn is a Nazi, with his ignorance, prejudices, and bullying:

What kind of a relationship is this where one party gives all the orders? "All right then if you don't do what I want I won't play." Tell him to go to hell — and if you won't I damned well will. Here and now take it from me that you have a perfect right to date and write anyone you like; and bear this mind too. There is only one person in the world who has the slightest shadow of right to give those orders to you and that's me. The fact that I haven't used that right and that it would be absurd to try and that I don't intend to use it is beside the point. Until I release you from the promises you made to me and you from mine to you, that right exists. Be yourself darling. If you don't care for me anymore, have some self-respect. What did you used to tell me about women who let themselves be their husband's door mats?

In his next letter he does not apologize, even though he realizes it must have caused her pain. He emerges from his battle station just long enough to say that he does appreciate Lynn's kindness to her. How bizarre, when he has just called him a Nazi storm trooper.

Three weeks later he receives a letter from her. He is reassured that she still needs him. She has somehow managed to convince him that she has remained fundamentally true to herself. He believes that this sets her apart from other women. And for this he loves her, as have the other men in her life. But he senses that Lynn knows her weak points and is using them to get what he wants. Tom sees this happening and is disturbed. He apologizes and comes around to the view that she is doing Lynn some good:

> *He demands more than anyone has a right to demand (nothing wrong with that – we all do) but as far as I can see gives nothing in return. You admit as much yourself when you analyse what married life with him would likely be. The fact that you who has a unique gift for it have distilled something enriching out of your relationship…you have done it every time with the most unpromising material. The point is – and you carefully underline this also – that Lynn is a hopeless mess emotionally and mentally.*

Paddy and Tom are surprisingly frank with each other about this relationship. He has no qualms about telling her what he thinks. On her side, she seems to be asking for his understanding. Or perhaps his evaluation. There are no secrets.

I return to the question of my own voyeurism. How much of this relationship with Lynn do I need to include here? Essentially, I want to know what happens between Paddy and Tom. Why did we not return to England? How and why did things deteriorate between them? Who did what to whom? Is there an obvious culprit? For now, the "Lynn situation" is center stage for them both. My mother is not making good decisions about her choice of a man. My father rides a roller coaster. He is torn between jealous anger and attempts at understanding.

So far I have not read ahead as I go through the letters. I simply take them day by day, year by year. I have family stories that have come down to me over the years, but they are two dimensional second hand, and come from the distance of time. Now I am walking beside my parents as they struggle with the war, their separation, their attempts at communication over a great distance. I will not find truth in a finite sense. But at least I have an unfolding story.

My friend, the one who wrote of memory loops, might view it this way. I am connecting to the memories, or in this case the words of someone else "in the hopes of glimpsing what once was real."

In a February letter he returns to the children, a happier subject:

What a way you have of describing things. I don't know how it is but just with a few simple words you make me see and hear the children with almost painful vividness. Big and strong and lovely are they? You bet they are. No children of yours could be anything else. I can just see Peter explaining to Felicity how water gets in the taps. Don't worry darling it won't do them any harm to work things out for themselves.

Then in March an odd passage crops up:

I am thinking in terms of seeing you this year. Not unreasonably I think because in spite of all the disaster in the Far East, we can, if we play our hand right, force victory over Germany this year. Then it won't be too difficult to settle Japan's hash. The logistic for this is a Second Front on the Continent this spring or summer to supply the anvil to the Red Army's hammer. It can be done simply because it must be done if Britain and British Empire is to survive in any shape.

The Red Army can beat Hitler on its own — there is little doubt of that.

He continues in this vein, losing himself in hypotheticals about the war. He also loses his idea that he will be seeing her. He says nothing more about it. He is fiercely passionate about the Red Army and quite derogatory at times about the British. The Americans don't figure in yet for him.

Scarcely a week later, he does an about-face. He has received her two letters of 15th and 25th February:

And they nearly pulled me in half. I'm seeing Bernard this weekend and I'll tell him just what I think of his lunacy. You must ON NO

ACCOUNT make plans to come back this summer if Christine won't sponsor you any longer. What about a job?

He is now much more pessimistic about the progress of the war. He believes that Russia can guarantee a victory in 1942 only if a Second Front is established in Europe. Otherwise, defeat is the only possible outcome:

Believe me darling, things are on a raw edge and whichever way they go there is going to be real privation over here for the first time.

He deplores what is happening in Britain. A creeping paralysis is at work. He sees no action, no attempt to "get a force over the Channel." Without this, he fears starvation within a year. But any action could lead to disaster:

As I see it things will reach their climax about the time you are talking of coming home – the Atlantic full of submarines and battleships, England on real "fortress" rations (to use the present pretty name for it) and victory or defeat a matter of weeks or even days. <u>You mustn't think of it.</u>

He has also given up his idea of coming to the U.S.A.:

That's not only a question of my not being able to get out of the country except on government service; if I could I wouldn't. I've a job to do here. This is my own country and my own people. I want to help with it for the principle I believe to be right and to see a better sort of England for Peter and Felicity to grow up in.

On the next page of his letter, he puts it back in her lap:

My own darling, I have told you as strongly as I know how not to come back and why not. But we took a chance on your going – maybe another one on your coming back would be justifiable. Make your own decision. There are even better reasons that I can see why you should come back than why you should stay. One thing only – wait till the autumn or else very early spring. Summer will be death on the Atlantic. Anyway time will help to make a decision for you. Victory this year, Paddy, this year.

He really does not know what to say, what to do. He cannot come down on one side or the other without the risk of doing the wrong thing. Sending us away may well have become the wrong thing. What is missing from this conversation is whether civilians could even make a transatlantic crossing in 1942. Tom doesn't seem to have given this any thought. Perhaps the obvious answer might be too much to bear. For now he can still live on hope.

April comes and he hasn't heard from her for over a month. He is very worried.

When he last heard from her she was talking about moving. Maybe that is it. Or it could be sunken ships, planes shot down. He is more certain than ever that she must not come back, nor must we children. Hitler is blitzing Britain again, this time on the small badly defended places. He fears Oxford may be next.

We haunt his sleep:

The most horrible nightmare I've ever had was the other night (not for the first time) when I dreamed you and the children were dead. I don't think any possibility frightens me so much. And six years ago I hadn't even met you – out of my thirty one years I've known you for about five and a half and out of these five and a half, we have been parted for nearly two. And yet you are more important to me than anything or anyone else I have ever known.

On other fronts, there are problems. The Dean and Christine can no longer support us. Tom is sending us sixteen pounds a month, about $70.00. There is mention that Paddy's visa will expire on July 31st of this year.

Finally he gets a cable from her as well as a letter that has taken three weeks to arrive. He learns that we have moved to Jacksonville Beach, Florida:

One thing is your new place must be absolutely ideal for the children. God how will they ever get used to the English climate again? Incidentally it's going to be fairly hot later on isn't it. Tell me more about it darling and don't forget snaps and (if possible) a movie film. How lovely they must be and how madly and badly I want to see them, badly as I want to see you.

But he doesn't want to hear more about Lynn.

I don't know if you deliberately bring Lynn to keep me up to scratch or what, but I'm afraid I shall never be able to judge him fairly – unless perhaps I have a chance to know him as well as you do. I've said quite enough about him so I won't say anymore now. But please don't tell me more than is absolutely necessary. I find – well, let it go. Sick was he? I'm not sure I'm not glad.

He continues to press her about getting a job in order to eliminate obligations to Christine. He expresses concern about her geographical location, fearing that stray submarines may be nearby "shelling bits of undefended coast for something to do."

He might have been even more worried had he known that we were kept from our beach one day by an oil slick from the sunken tanker, "GulfAmerica." Torpedoed by a German U-Boat, it was split in half off neighboring Ponte Vedra Beach.

His mood changes. He and Bernard spend some good time together:

I took him up to London with me for two days. We did the following things. First of all, the weather was glorious – we've suddenly dropped into a real heat wave, smashing sunshine all day long and long warm veiled nights with enough light at midnight almost to read by. I finished my jobs early on Wednesday and, as we finished near there, we took a boat on the river near Windsor and bashed and sculled up and down lazily, looked at Magna Carta island....

He casually mentions that he has met a woman during his work journeys to London. He and Bernard give her a ride home, but he doesn't say from where. She gives them tea and entertains them until Bernard's train to Tern Hill leaves at 2 a.m.

I pause, for this is important news. Do I time-travel into the future, revealing what I came to know of Esther Mizel? Or do we simply join Tom and Bernard, drinking tea at her house late at night? I decide not to rush ahead:

She is somebody I met fairly recently and is rather nice. 30 with a daughter 10 years old, husband in the Middle East, living on Rose Hill with her sister, brother-in-law, all refugees from London where they had a terrific bashing. A full two days. Incidentally about Esther M, Bernard said thoughtfully later, "I don't think I'll tell Paddy too much about today. She might scent a 'case'. If you do, darling – there isn't one. Just that. Nor did anything happen – we just had some tea and talked. Rather like we used to do at No. 7.

That's all for now. We glimpse Esther in the wings, unsure of what her role will be or if she will even make it onto the stage.

A month later he writes again:

Well my darling I have now seen the best movie film ever made and I don't mean maybe. It arrived yesterday just before I was finishing this letter so I held it over till I'd seen it.

Darling, I don't know what to say. I always thought you were these pretty good people but just exactly how smashing I never realised.

The Florida film has arrived. My father has it in his hands. Until now it has simply been a cherished little bit of visual history which I retrieved from the clutter of his belongings after his death in 1994. My husband had it transferred to CD Rom. After seven decades the colors are still miraculously bright. Now, though, as I read Tom's words, time twists and tangles between past and present, between him and me. It feels like a collision. For I remember this beach that is in the film, the water, the Florida sun which burned me so badly. He is seeing me there. We come together in a way that is difficult to grasp but feels like a reunion nonetheless.   He takes us in one by one:

First you. My dear you have changed as I knew you and hoped you would. You have become more poised and sure of yourself – there's confidence in every bit of your face now and it's the same funny face I love so much with all the features fitting into that bloody attractive whole so odd and yet so rightly in the way Ive never been able to explain. And your figure my sweet is marvelous. It always was good but you seem to be more orthodox and do your bathing dress and frock (I love that one with the green and big white patches) show if off right? You're lovely all of you and I'm at once proud of knowing you're my wife and jealous of anyone who can see you when I can't and madly badly wanting you and wanting this bloody war to be over so that I can have you again.

Felicity. There's no doubt that she's going to be Paddy No. 2. She's well on the way already. God what a lovely child! And (I don't suppose you need telling) doesn't she know it. Now I've seen her pigtails and the little bit (thank you darling) where she lets her hair down. I can see how right you were to do it that way. And the saucy capers and faces she pulls!

Peter. This isn't quite his picture, is it? The two women steal it. Especially as he looks in a pretty bad temper in his only close-up. But for the sheer grace of movement he's got both of you beaten easily and that's saying a good deal. I'm thinking of when you put on his bathing drawers and he sends like silent lightening into the sea.

We live for him in these few brief moments, active and beautiful. But silent.

He finishes this letter with a warning. He has heard on the BBC that some saboteurs landed from a U boat at Jacksonville Beach and were rounded up by the FBI. He feels quite uneasy but tries to be lighthearted:

Are you sure you're alright where you are? Anyway, I hope someone has given you a revolver and taught you how to use it if any stray Nazis do land from rubber boats at the bottom of your garden don't hesitate at all …

The Transatlantic mails have slowed down. He receives her June 1ˢᵗ letter on July 5ᵗʰ. His letters to her are now only monthly. He carries them with him, adding bits when he has a chance - -in a train station waiting room or a London hotel. His work keeps him busy and on the move. Their conversation is becoming stretched, their connection more attenuated. Lynn still creeps in, unwanted. Tom admits to having been quite dense about Paddy's reasons for staying in Jacksonville. It finally dawns on him that Lynn is there.

In early August, he pleads again for her return, but this time it is not a longing of fantasy. He calls to her patriotism. He believes he has the British government behind him:

One or two things have happened which I expect alter the situation. First there is the appeal by the government to British subjects to come home. This isn't a bluff. Quite frankly we are in a desperate position. There is one hope only – and thank God it's a pretty big hope – which is complete mobilization of the people for the opening of the Second Front, both to see that it is opened at all, and to see that it's done properly when it is.

Don't think that this doesn't mean you because it does. It means every manjack of us because what we've had up to now is a fleabite to what we're going to get if the German armies manage to get through to the Caucasus through our procrastination and passivity.

I'm putting it quite straight to you darling because I know you'd rather have it that way. Its your war and my war now and we can't argue the toss about it any more. It's life or death for both of us and for the twins even more than us.

You must take the choice of sacrificing some of the joy you have of them now or of all the future you and I may be able to have together. Any

future in the way of whether they are to become useful citizens in a pro-
gressive sensible society or to become lifelong members of a bread line.
Whether they may grow up into fascists themselves –
*   Yes, it's as sharp as that – how do you think Hitler produced his SS?*
Education and environment, nothing else.

I find this vague and confusing. Is there to be a peoples' revolution, Russian
style, with armbands, slogans, and marching to the barricades? Is she supposed to come back somehow, risky though it would be, to join in? And what
about the children? He implies our absence but he doesn't come up with suggestions about our care. He says that next winter and spring could be equally
as bad in the United States as in Britain. Then the clincher. The British
government is now paying all return fare.

She obviously doesn't bite for, by the time he sends his next letter in early
September, there is no mention of her return. In fact, he seems to be replacing
us. He is acquiring a family of sorts. He is staying often on his London trips
with Esther's family. The children there lead him to thoughts of us:

I can look at them (the three girls) and make guesses as to which Felicity
will be most like when she comes back. Peter I have to imagine.

He returns to "our fight, the fight of the ordinary people." He is not going to
let her off the hook. She must fight as well and think whether she is doing her
part. His resentment and his disappointment in her are beginning to emerge,
little weeds growing in the garden of his previous adoration. He attacks her
mothering:

Many English mothers have learned that they aren't indispensable to
their children and have learned a new responsibility to the community
at large – and learned to enjoy it. I'm not trying to be pompous but I
do know now that there are better ways of enjoying yourself than bask-
ing in the sun and that someone's company is hardly worth having if it
has to be washed down with a quart of whiskey. In fact I'll be quite
blunt with you, I think you're wasting yourself and wasting your time,

and the children as an excuse won't hold water because (a) children are perfectly happy wherever they are (b) the weather you describe is tropical weather which is definitely not good for children. The answer is as before; get a job; and get it in some other part of America. Go East young woman, try Vermont or Massachusetts or New York State. Get about a bit if you do nothing else.

This passage is astonishing in its insensitivity. Most glaring is his utter lack of understanding of what children need. We are simply sidebars to the main story, obliviously happy in the midst of our disrupted lives, splashing in the Florida ocean-- an ocean alive with enemy submarines and a beach recently desecrated by oil from the sunken tanker. My memory of that day has stayed with me always: clear, dramatic, and subtly threatening. He further reduces his argument to trivial comments about the weather. He is an expert, it seems, on the tropics and childrens' health. I need only look at the Florida 8 mm film to know that children are, in fact, not happy wherever they are. My brother Peter shows himself to be a sullen, angry child, refusing to engage with the camera or the person behind it.

I will take my father to task even further here. Does he really think that Paddy has such freedom of movement as his advice implies? From a strictly practical point, travel takes money. Which she does not have. This he knows. He can be forgiven for his lack of geographical perspective in far-ranging suggestions about where she might go. England is a small place; that is his frame of reference. You can go about hither and thither with relative ease in short amounts of time. Not so North America, even if you shrink it down to the East Coast.

Fundamentally, though, he is criticizing what he perceives to be her lack of initiative. But I would imagine that getting through every day as a single mother with two very young children, no money, war on, and the future bleak, takes the kind of initiative that he could not envision. She is not on tour. She is trying to survive. He does not like Lynn and disapproves of her relationship with him. All he really knows is that Paddy has picked him up in Tennessee where his English parents are neighbors of Christine. His jealousy, which is quite understandable, is undermining his belief in her. He does not spare her his blunt truth.

Three weeks later he writes again. He and Paddy have been discussing the war and politics. Their views diverge. Anger is evident on both sides. He acknowledges the frustrations of what he calls "this long range argument where it takes anything up to two months to get a reaction from a statement made." In her letters, she has made it clear that she doesn't like what she calls his superior attitude and constant criticism of everything and everyone who doesn't agree with him. He is hard, intolerant. He admits that he is and has always been, is worse now. He speaks of being ashamed till it hurts to read in the papers every day of what the Red Army is doing in Stalingrad, to know that the Russians are calling more desperately every day for a Second Front. She has accused him of being inconsistent, of making incorrect predictions. She has also said that she wouldn't like to live under Communism. He replies:

> *Here's one prediction I'll stick to because it isn't a prediction it's a simple fact: after this war England at any rate and America probably will have no choice beyond the two – communism or fascism. Maybe communism without Bolsheviks and the OGPU, maybe fascism without brown or black shirts, but communism or fascism nonetheless. There is not a third way now and it will be one of those two however they're dressed up and whatever they are called. I'm sorry if you don't like the prospect but that's what it is; because capitalism in Europe can only survive another holocaust like this one by using machine guns; and that's fascism; or it will be overthrown and when it is it will be replaced by communism. You needn't believe me if you don't want to – but at least keep this letter and check up in a few years time.*

She did keep this letter. More than a few years have passed. Enough said. It would seem that she at least has won this argument.

Two months later they take off their gloves and return to their corners. Things are more peaceful. He agrees with her that he has been judging her by standards he shouldn't have used. "England after three years of war is a very different place from America after less than one." He suggests they return to themselves, their relationship, their future.

She has asked him a question about divorce which he says he doesn't really understand:

Of course I'm not indifferent about divorce but I think that it is not a step which should be even contemplated without very careful consideration and discussion where there are children involved. For instance, in our case, I wouldn't even think of it until we had a chance to meet again and really determine how we felt about each other.... My dear it is two and half years since we saw each other; we have been leading utterly different lives. It would not be reasonable to expect either of us not to make other relationships.

He is preparing her for his next piece of news. He has found someone, a good friend, a companion and "someone who loves me as much as you do."

I find it odd that he thinks he can know how much someone loves him. Does he think love can be quantified, its volume calculated, allowing it to be measured against another love? In some way perhaps this is meant to reassure Paddy. Or is it a challenge? He describes the woman, Esther, as "someone whose love I can repay – not by giving her anything that is yours but by giving her some of the things I have to give." Does he keep his loves in little compartments, each with its own inventory?

He describes Esther, her shape, size, eye color, hair texture (curly and red). He couldn't really call her good looking and her figure is not as good as Paddy's:

But she has something of your power of impressing her personality on everything she does and says and so being <u>alive</u>.

He refers to her unhappy marriage:

Some of the things he didn't give her I can – affection, belief in herself and the realization that she is a woman as good as most other women. In other words to smash down her inferiority complex. That's something you wouldn't understand fully darling because you never had an inferiority complex of that kind. And she has repaid me by loving me.

Now where does this lead me?

It leads him to a most unexpected place. I am now face to face with the origins of an oft-repeated family story. Here it is in his words:

> *I don't think to any impasse. When the time comes to make a choice for you and her, I want to know that you are both strong enough to make that choice independent of me. It will be enough for me to know that I have done the main job I have tried to do — make you both richer and stronger for having known me, as Christ knows both of you have in your different ways made me the richer and stronger for having known you. I have no feelings of guilt towards either of you, as I now understand you have none towards me. But I am sincerely and deeply sorry that I didn't appreciate to the full at the time the circumstances that made your decisions in regard to Lynn so much more difficult than mine with Esther.*

There is much to parse in this passage. It is not clear what he actually means. Is each to make her own decision whether she wants him or not? Is this a decision each will be capable of making because of the ways in which he has strengthened and enriched them? What if they both want him? He certainly has a very high opinion of himself. In sum, he absolves himself from any responsibility for the outcome. He will leave it to them to decide. He then answers Paddy's unasked question. He has known Esther for six months, but "there have only been about three months of serious developments." He expresses some concern about the effect this news will have on her. He is not afraid. He is being straight with her, as she has been about Lynn.

He concludes by saying that he hopes he hasn't spoiled her Christmas. Have the children received the Christmas books and did we like them? I wonder if he ever wrote to us. There are no cards or letters. We are five years old now, no longer the toddlers who departed his life so suddenly. He sometimes tries to find us in other children our age, a sad little act of ineffective shapeshifting.

This November letter, with news of Esther, is the last one of 1942. On our side, we are still in Florida. There are changes ahead.

CHAPTER 18

1943

I TALK WITH FRIENDS AT times about my memoir. They ask, "How far have you gotten?" They seem to expect a chronology of my life laid out in orderly steps, year by year, decade after tedious decade, with a beginning, a middle, and an end. A boring resume of all the things I have and have not done. I try to explain myself. I want them to know that this memoir is not a life calendar filled with dates and years. Rather, it is a collection of memories which I weave as a write. The weaving becomes a tapestry. This is my war story. For five years war defines my life and for the years to come. It defines my mother's life, my brother's life, my father's life. The war lives alongside us and we live alongside it. We are never far from its push and pull, even on the most ordinary days. The war forces decisions. It ruptures loving relationships. We must form new ones. My parents choose other partners to ease their loneliness. Across the thousands of miles of our separation we are learning to live in new ways in new places. As the war moves, so do we. What happened when? Where were we? I need a chronology of our wartime life that does not rely solely on my own childish memory and stories from my mother. My father's letters are a fragile spine of passing time. They help me shape my story.

It is January, 1943. Peter and I are now five years old. On January 5, Paddy's 29th birthday, Tom writes his first letter of the year. He hasn't heard from her for weeks. Where are we, he wonders. Mum (Paddy's mother) and Mummy (his mother) have received cards from her posted in Norfolk, Virginia. He is surprised because he thought we were going to Massachusetts.

I am blindsided. Norfolk has never figured in my storytelling. I thought we had gone directly to Minnesota from Florida. Now I see that we have camp-followed Lynn to his naval base. I try to imagine myself in this picture. All I can find is one small memory scrap. I am standing in a cafeteria line pushing a metal tray along a counter. I am fascinated by the tray's sections, one for each item of food. I am living my life in sections. What did I do with my Florida life? Block it out forever? Is this how five year old children cope with constant change and unpredictability? Life becomes a series of doors closing behind us. The present quickly replaces the past. The past becomes irrelevant. There is no need of it. I have no memory of life in Norfolk.

In this same letter Tom gives her an update on his finances. He hopes she has received the 20 pounds he sent at Christmas, 18 from him which he has saved up, and two pounds from her mother. But he is concerned about the future. He may be called up. She must keep looking for a way to earn some money.

He spends Christmas with Esther's family. He goes to the movies. He gives Paddy a detailed critique of "Mrs. Miniver," one of two films she recommended. Mrs. M goes on his chopping block:

> *Before I start I'll make it clear that I would probably be more lenient if I were in exile – although I don't think that applies to Mrs. Miniver. So don't think I'm knocking you or your taste in films. I can see why you liked them all right and I understand, but here is what I thought of them.*

What follows is four pages of criticism. His teaching moment begins as a reality check on life during the war but it eventually turns into a passionate diatribe on the evils of class. Poor Mrs. Miniver goes to buy a hat not knowing that he will soon knock it right from her head:

> *My darling were you buying hats in late August 1939. Do you think anyone worth tuppence was: I can tell you one thing for certain – those who were still are. And what effect did the war have on Mrs. Miniver? None at all that I could see; she started with her mouth open like a codfish*

and a misty look in her eye and finished in the same condition....The film covered a period when every country in Europe had been overrun by Hitler, when the Polish, French, and British armies had been defeated and decimated, when British workers were sweating twelve and fourteen hours a day to repair the disaster <u>caused</u> by the Mrs. Minivers who by their birth, upbringing and own opinion should have been leading the nation but instead preferred to buy hats and run flower shows. None of that was mentioned of course. These people have done very nicely out of life – what did they put back into it? ...These people aren't England and thank God for it.

He gets Paddy's Christmas letter from Norfolk which took six weeks to reach him. He says he has been in a fog about her movements and has waited to hear her new address. In her letter she gives him a dig in the ribs and he must reply:

But please don't say things like my despising people who aren't as busy as I am. If I ever do it will be a sign that its time I gave it up as under those conditions nothing I did could have any useful results at all. You see the key of my work and beliefs is that I believe in <u>people</u>, what people think and do are the only real things in life.

I wonder who his people are. He has lived a privileged life in a comfortable town surrounded by family and the luxuries of a first class education. Does he long for more grit, more harsh reality to give him legitimacy as a participant in the peoples' revolution to come? He writes about history, its progressive nature, stages of civilization, Lincoln and Washington and John Donne, humanity, the limits of religion, all wrapped up together in fine language and noble thoughts. He is an idealistic man, drawing on his intellect and his great facility with language, writing in the midst of war to his absent wife and children. As I read, I wonder where is the feeling? He has just learned where we are and this is what she gets. Finally he comes back to earth and apologizes for his "damned lecture."

He is hearing about the farm for the first time. He has concerns, fearing that the woman who has agreed to take us in could turn out to be another Christine. He returns to previous admonitions:

And although again I understand your feelings you must realize that you are not indispensable to the children and I can still see no reason why you can't get them looked after and go to work. Its difficult – of course it is – you know me well enough I think to realize that I don't advise the easy way out of things and to know why I don't.

What does he mean by "indispensable"? I think this must be an English idea. The less you give to your children, the more they will do for themselves? My mother is our lifeline. We have no one but her as she flounders and struggles and makes mistakes and shows courage in the midst of this terrible situation. She is virtually homeless, dependent on the kindness of strangers for her survival.

He cannot be blamed for his lack of understanding. Nor can she be blamed for not understanding how he is living. How can they understand each other? Their letters are becoming more infrequent. The war goes on, its dark power filling their lives with uncertainty and unpredictability. My father repeatedly reminds her that any decisions about their future must wait until the war is over.

She writes and now he knows where we are. We are in a Minnesota winter living with the Wyatts on their dairy farm:

Well, you do move around don't you? Where you are now sounds an ideal spot for the children; I hope you will find it one too. I gave you my advice in a recent letter – I wonder if you got it? – it was to go to a town and take a job (did you guess?). I can only say now that I hope I was wrong and I hope you will be really happy. This depends of course on the Wyatts to some extent; but if you are really able now to live an independent full life cut off from contact with people of your own age and interests then I am very proud of you – because to succeed in this job is the biggest test you could have set for yourself.

She has moved out of desperation. This is not a test that she has designed for herself. A friend of Lynn, a fellow sailor, has told his parents in Minnesota of our plight and his mother has responded. We go by train, a journey that has no place in my memory. I can only imagine.

Tom wants to support her choice but try as he might he cannot resist letting her know what she is missing. There are a lot of "if's" in his response. If she can do this, he is proud of her. But he would rather see her living in his picture, surrounded by like minded friends, his real people, in a town enjoying the fruits of meaningful work. Again, we cannot blame him. How could he envision her life? She has agreed to help the Wyatts on the farm in exchange for room and board. She is to bake bread, chop wood, and help with other chores. It is February in Minnesota. Snow and cold and the hardships of rural life in winter are what we know. The farm help has dwindled as the young men have all gone off to the war. Margaret Wyatt is the local schoolteacher and we go to her one room schoolhouse. Our father doesn't comment on this beginning of our American education. He may not even know.

On the war front, he tells her that the battle of Stalingrad has been over for nearly a week. A Second Front may be imminent. There are rumors that Hitler may be either dead or mad. He has received a letter from her. It is hard to tell from what he says initially, but it seems that she has again raised the question of divorce. As always, we see her only through the veil of his response:

> *I have had your letter for nearly a week. I have been thinking about it most of the time, trying to decide whether my first reactions were correct — because, as you should realize, a discussion that goes 5,000 miles isn't one that should be taken lightly or hastily. On the whole, I think they were and that is not surprising to me as I have been thinking quite a lot about this business for a great deal longer than a week — in fact practically since you went away and I first settled down to the realization that it would be a very long time before we saw one another again, if at all.*

He reviews their relationship. He begins with all the good things they have done for each other. But soon he recounts what is lacking. He is hard on her:

You are my equal and I do not recognize any voluntary relationship that is not between equals. Because you differed on that basic fact, because your life has been serial story of men on whom you have leant and depended, this has happened. And because you have never faced your own problems squarely because you have never, in spite of your continual quest for knowledge and happiness, looked in the only right pace, inside <u>yourself</u>, you have found the easy way out each time, using your own great gifts not consciously selfishly, for you have enriched all the men you have known and me most of all, but unconsciously to attract to you some person who provides a temporary solution – but it isn't a solution at all really, it is in each case an escape.

I could be angry with him for throwing this at her when she is down and out. But he is not far off the mark. She once said to me, when I was old enough to become her confidante, that whenever things had felt hopeless, someone turned up to help her out. She didn't say a man, but this is what she meant. He tells her that immediate divorce is no out. Lynn has gone away. She is merely changing one absentee husband for another.

He cites hard facts, like it or not, which she must recognize. He beats the drums of the war again:

You have never even tried to raise discussion on the things I say about the war although I purposely make them provocative. But I see why now. The war doesn't interest you; it is a nuisance and you are sorry about the bombing, and that, but what it really means is that Lynn has had to go away and you wanted him very badly. You don't see it as we do – a fight between WE and THEY, a fight to decide whether we shall have a house or job or a right to any decision at all except that of the Jews or the Poles or the White Russians; die of starvation or just die.

The war, my dear, is at the moment the only really real thing in the world, and every one of our personal problems is subject to the overriding answer to this main question.

She is flunking out. She must stand on her own two feet, take a real job, in the real world with real people. She is talking divorce. He hits back:

Try to face the real facts of divorce now not as a magical and painless way out, the exchanging of a man of whom you've grown tired for another of who you haven't yet, but as a tedious, disgraceful and unsatisfactory process in the English courts, at the end of which you would have lost me with no surety of gaining anything in return: Perhaps not Lynn and certainly not your own freedom.

I wonder what she has been telling him about her life. Does she tell him about the wood chopping and the baking? Does he know anything about the one room school house, our lessons, how we are doing in this snowy world? So far my brother and I have been lingering safely in the shadows of their written exchanges. We are there to be kissed at the end of a letter. We are delightful in a photo or a film. Tom expresses occasional concern about our education and the threat to our Englishness as we live this American life. Now our father brings us front and center:

And there is one point on which your lack of clear thinking has led you into a real black out as far as the realities of our situation go; that is, the children. Some time ago when all this came up before, you said you promised to be "generous with them" if you were divorced. Surely you must realize that I could not willingly permit a man whom Ive never met nor had a letter from but who I have only reason to regard as an ignorant, conceited young bounder without self-respect or self control to become the father of my children? And don't you think it is a bit cool to promise to be generous with something that is not yours to be generous with? Thank you for nothing. The facts are these — I have an equal right with you to determine the future of our children, and if we cannot agree by reasonable discussion on this, then it will of course rest with the courts to award custody. At the present if I was forced to take any action I should divorce you and claim (and get) legal custody, because it is a matter of deep concern to me that my children should grow up to a full, frank and open knowledge of life, a life which I can hardly see them getting in the USA.

He finishes, but not with love:

I have said nothing about love in this letter. From what you say it is plain to me that you have no love for me, so it would be out of place. I can see that you love Lynn and that he loves you, and I hope that he comes back safely, and that you both will gain a truer realization of what is going on in the world and that you will base your decisions on that.
    Always, Tom

He avoids his usual goodbye. He omits "Your loving husband."

It is April. At the Wyatt's farm we are waiting for spring. Tom is sorry that he has not written sooner. He has been thinking about what he has said. He walks back into his previous letter:

I had to write you a striker last time – not because I wanted to but because you were due for a kick in the pants and I was the one who had to deliver it. This wasn't nice for me I can assure you but it was the way it had to be.

She has hurt him, accusing him of being conceited and not giving a damn about the children. In spite of this, he tenders an apology of sorts.

It may surprise you for instance to know that I don't get a great deal of occasion for sitting down and thinking out my personal problems, and it would have been better for you if I had had less time to…This is not something to my credit and your discredit; its just a natural result of the different lives we have led for three years. I am to blame very greatly in not having made sufficient allowance for this; I am also very much to blame in expecting automatically that you would accept my way of looking at the war and what it means to people like us just because I told you so….

But he cannot let her off the hook. He must maintain the moral high ground:

This isn't to say that I don't hold you responsible for what has happened to you at least to a major extent. You have no excuse for becoming so completely Americanised in all the wrong directions. You have no excuse for becoming anti Semitic, anti-British (you are though you don't know it yet), anti-Soviet in fact anti-everything that Lynn is anti-. I can remember and I can find your first letter to me about Lynn. It was a good clear letter and you put your finger on his weaknesses, his conceit his intolerance and ignorance. And since that time I have seen every one of those qualities appearing in you. I made a great mistake which was undoubtedly due to conceit; I thought I could fight him alone just by correspondence when he carried all the guns and all the advantages. It was a big mistake but I hope its not too late to learn from it and correct it.

Who is supposed to learn? Himself? Her? I wonder what he has in mind. Had he actually written to Lynn? I imagine Lynn backstage, jauntily dressed in his naval uniform, handsome, seductive, and stupid. Lynn surely would not have taken pen to paper to respond to any correspondence from Tom. He is all right where he is. He has the goods. Why would he expose himself by coming front and center? He exists only in Paddy's narrative. He has no speaking part of his own.

Tom then does a turnaround. He attempts to rationalize the hard line he is taking. He does think there is a possibility that they could live again together happily. Otherwise he would not be going to such lengths to whip her into shape.

He reverts to a chat mode, if anything he approaches can ever be reduced to simple chat. She has asked about rationing. He educates her with a two-page treatise on the subject. He is curious about Minneapolis, which he terms an "American provincial city." How does it compare to Oxford? Has she been to the Minneapolis Symphony yet? He has gone to the London Philharmonic, has seen a good film about the blitz. He has given blood.

But soon he returns to his admonitions. This time he hits very close to home, literally:

> *Lastly there is one point I want to bring out quite strongly and it's the only other one on which I want to make my position quite unambiguous. It concerns your mother. As you know she is getting old although she is still marvelously active and as bright and lively as ever. If I said the prospect of seeing you and the children again was the only thing that was keeping her going I would be exaggerating; but I would not if I said that if she knew of the position between us or of your intention not to come back to England it would deal her a blow from which she would never recover completely. Further to this if you still think that in certain eventualities you can "go to your mother" you must think again; she's done her job by you and the least you can do is to let her do what she wants to — end her life in peace and happiness, knowing that you are happy — and as you ought to know your mother is plenty sensible enough to realize that that is something that doesn't depend on who you happen to be living with, but on you. Even if you aren't happy, you must make her think you are; and if, in certain eventualities, you think your life is shipwrecked she must never know it. The one thing that really would make me lose all my respect for you would be if (supposing) you wouldn't have me and Lynn wouldn't have you or if one or both of us were killed you went home to her instead of facing things out yourself. Remember this — if things work out so that you marry Lynn I shall simply say that this is what will make you happy, and that's something I don't believe. The rest is up to you.*

This is strong stuff. Paddy is a threat to her mother's well being. Tom has become very close to "Mum" and quite rightly wants to spare her injury. His language, however, betrays him. He may well be motivated by compassion for the elderly mother. But in his choice of words he cannot avoid expressing the anger he feels toward her daughter.

He closes with a note, an after thought at the end of his letter:

P.S. It may help you to appreciate my point of view when I tell you this — not to scare you or upset you or make out Im the hell of a fellow but just to show how we normally live; I had lunch a few weeks ago in the restaurant in a big department store (not in London — in a town about the size of Oxford) ; at tea time a sneak raider came in at 50 feet and blew it to bits including the waitresses who had served my lunch.

Tom chooses lunch rather than afternoon tea. He is spared. The waitresses, however, have no choice. War is fickle in its destructiveness.

As I continue reading my father's letters, I see that my parents' relationship has many facets, not all of which have to do with angry recriminations against undesirable lovers. My mother always possessed intellectual curiosity in spite of having to leave school at the age of fifteen. She gave me a complete Random House dictionary as a gift. It is large and hard-backed, a great tome. She loved to look things up. Now she draws on Tom for knowledge, as she has done in the past. Is the Prime Minister elected by the House of Lords, she asks. No, darling, he is not and he is not elected at all. He continues with a clear and detailed explanation of the structure and processes of the British Government. She is beginning her job at the Consulate in St. Paul and she wants to know her employers. She asks and he delivers. He treats her request with respect. He gives her his time and his thoughts.

It is May, 1943, and the war is beginning to turn. British troops have entered Tunis. The RAF are blasting Germany, repayment for London, Coventry, Plymouth.

Every night now we hear the going over — and while the air shakes we feel this is it at last. This is victory on the march. We are righting at last. The baby killers are being killed, its all been worth it. But there's nothing that can stop us now and the people know it. And I think also everyone is genuinely glad that Yanks did so well after their early misadventures. I know I am.

He returns to "us." We hear her voice again in his reply. She has returned to the subject of divorce. He reminds her that he has already made his feelings clear. He adds that she had first spoken of it over a year ago, before he had ever met Esther:

> *Its not an easy course to take, to hold one's future suspended and just concentrate on a day-to-day job, but its not so bad when you get stuck into it — most of the time anyway. Youre reproaching me in that statement I know; because you and Lynn found things hellish (it was worse than hellish in the London blitzes and at Sevastopol) you thought there was something I could have done to help and I didn't do it. Believe me there was nothing at all. If you and Lynn are to find any real happiness together you must learn to face reality for yourselves...This is the first crisis in your life you are having to face entirely alone. I'll help you all I can but the main effort can only come from you.*

He is a father talking to a troublesome child. I do not hear a man in conversation with his wife, the mother of his children whose desperate situation has come about wholly as the result of his decision to send them away. He finds it in himself to support her but there is always a caveat, the little dig:

> *And I would like to say at this point that you have made a good start; Im glad youre busy on the farm and Im glad youre likely to get a job at the consulate. I know it isn't every body who can go into a factory. All I want to know is that you are doing work which interests you, brings you into contact with other people, and helps the war effort; and enables you to send the children to school.*

In a subsequent letter, he revisits the factory:

> *One last final word about factories. Yes I would like to see you in a factory, because that is where a strong young woman with your organizing ability, common sense and physical cleverness can do the best job. But you*

can also do a good job where you are, and youre happy where you are; so Im glad and happy that that's the way it is. But if it was only because this job was easier and more pleasant than that then I would still criticise anybody including myself. But doing a good job is the main thing isn't it?

I ask myself what is the main thing indeed. Must everything conform to his utopian vision of the future, a worker's world of Communist perfection? I suffer here from benefit of hindsight, of course. Her job at the consulate was not only a life-saver then, but she turned it into a great professional achievement in the twenty six years she was there. Tom is trying to be helpful and supportive but he damns with faint praise. It seems that nothing she does will ever be quite good enough. His ideals dim his humanity.

He gets news of her move to St. Paul and her new job--not from her, but from a letter she has written to her mother. Although she has not written to directly him, he still must comment:

You certainly seem to have made a very good job and I am pleased and I congratulate you. But get this quite straight; if you have done this please me (I don't think you have) I would not be so pleased at all; but you if have done it because you saw the necessity of it I am very pleased; because I have known your capabilities better than you and I have expected higher things of you than you have yourself.

He seems genuinely favorable toward her but cannot say it without qualification. I can imagine, however, that he may feel a sense of relief. She is working, we are in school. Peter and I now come back on stage. The grown ups can deal with their problems at another time. Tom has received "snaps" of us and a gramophone record:

I have had from you (i) the latest snaps of the children (ii) the gramophone record. I don't know which to start on. Every time I see a new picture of the children I get a new shock. I wonder if you can appreciate what they mean to me and to all of us, to see these vast changes each time. Of course I don't suppose you notice them being with them all the time but believe me when I think of the two little toddlers who went away I find it difficult to link them up with the smashing little boy and girl I see now. And isn't it amazing the way they are so definitely becoming Tom2 and Paddy2? In looks anyway – Peter seems to have much more of a Dubber [Paddy's family] temperament – although I can see myself in the keen interest he takes in things – and Felicity you in her interest in people. And I see a marked resemblance facially to my mother – although very very subordinate to you.

As for the record! First of all its nearly worn out already although I have very carefully passed a box of fibre needles around with it – so I'll want another sometime please (but only when you can afford it!) Peter hasn't changed much has he – his impulsiveness and quickness burst right through all the time – I especially like his interruptions (a)"to tell them about the heifers : (b) his "aah" to a remark of Felicity's on the other side (which Im sorry to say I can't understand). But what I liked best were the asides – especially Felicity's "but I cant keep from coughing" and "youre hurting me!"

Peter has been a Minnesota farm boy for a few months now, long enough to know where drama is found. He is excited. He wants his listeners to get the whole story. As for me, I am fighting Peter's attacks already. I wonder that my father found my plea so appealing.

Tom hears our voices. He is relieved to discover that we have not acquired unpleasant accents. Peter has only an American intonation but I have quite a Southern drawl. I am alarmed to learn this. Perhaps my musical ear picks up accents quickly.

Tom goes on with bad news. He will not be "called up" to fight after all. He has been judged Grade 4 because of poor vision. He feels angry and personally insulted. He is sure that the only work he will have will be "to dig bloody latrines and make roads." His fierce desire to defend his country will pass unnoticed when the books are written.

He rises above it. He still has fantasies of a post war trip to the United States. He has received her post card showing the skyscraper where she works in downtown St. Paul. He imagines arriving after the war and throwing a stone at her window.

He ends more lovingly than in recent letters:

Good bye for now my dear. Look after yourself and the children. Give them my love and some big kisses, work hard, and the war will be over soon.

Tom writes again in July. He is very glad she likes her job and that we are happy in school. The war news is improving. Caution has been his watchword in any discussions about their future. Now, however, he cannot resist opening up that door a little crack:

I'm keeping very fit, working very hard, and in general not finding enough time to worry seriously about my personal problems. I hope it's the same with you; because we cant solve them till after the war. You do realize that now, don't you? Im looking forward very much to seeing you again. (Yes I permit myself that luxury for the first time in three years!) and the children, finding out again what sort of people you've become and interested too to know what youll think of me. Ive got a feeling we're both due to have quite a number of preconceptions broken up. The basic thing is to realize it; then you can take it, whatever that may be.

He seems to feel a small lifting of the burden of our absence, for he has been carrying us with him. For his own survival, however, he has kept an emotional distance. He has no control over physical distance. His letters to Paddy have alleviated this to some degree. They are in touch with each other. But he can only get to us, the children, through her. She sends photos and gramophone records, little faces and little voices seen and heard in snatches over a great distance. But I imagine these images and sounds have become

faint to him by now. I wonder again how often he may have questioned himself. Did we really have to go?

September arrives and with it a letter Paddy had posted on June 27th. This
is the first letter Tom has received from her since she moved to St. Paul. Her
mother has received two. Again he asks her to "let sleeping dogs lie" until the
end of the war. But she wants the dogs to get up and move. She prods him
with questions about the future. How can they have a useful conversation
about this or anything else? Tom writes in frustration:

> *It should be plain to you by now that we have been living such entirely*
> *different lives for over three years – now that we have changed into two*
> *different people; what is more we are quite unable to keep each other*
> *posted as to the directions we are taking due to the bad mail service. It*
> *is consequently quite impossible to carry on a connected correspondence*
> *when anything up to three months may elapse between asking a question*
> *and getting the answer; and since neither of us know the sort of life the*
> *other is leading we can only report in general terms and make in return*
> *very general observations.*

He reveals, however, that he has a plan "tucked away in a pigeon hole of my
mind" to come the USA for six months or so at the end of the war to see the
"sort of life she has been leading." They could get reacquainted. They could
share common ground. Decisions about their future might then flow more
easily. But he quickly rejects her attempt to gild the lily:

> *Nor have I any need to start what you call a "fresh life." The life I am*
> *leading now has no doubt many defects and weaknesses but it has reality*
> *and continuity, it is one in which I am able to fulfill myself more com-*
> *pletely than I have ever known before; I have already started the "fresh*
> *life" I want.*

Does he realize what he has said? It is a life without her. It is hard to
believe that he has not already made a decision. Esther scarcely appears

in his conversations with Paddy these days. Yet she is center stage in her play within a play. She is living in Oxford now. He is renting her two rooms in the house he owns, the house we lived in as a family before we left England. She appears briefly as a pronoun. Paddy has sent candy from us, "from the children":

> *Well you must tell the children what we did with the candy. We divided it up and shared it among the children down the road...They all said "thank you" to the children. I wonder if they remember any of them?*

Who are the "we?" "We" must be a couple. The image flows naturally from his pen. Although he still lives with his mother at the other end of the Lyndworth Close, he and Esther have become very much a part of each other's lives.

He goes back to the future. The war is pressing my parents but in an entirely different way now. They see that it will really come to an end. The rupture of evacuation, the years of separation, the coping, the loneliness on his side, the desperation on hers are being replaced by new anxieties. They are treading on fresh ground. Will they find a common path or will their ways diverge? Can they really trust each other? He is doubtful. He questions her motivation for suggesting that he put his name on list to immigrate to America:

> *If you are truthful with yourself I think you will realize that this proposal has from your end, one main object — to enable you to go on living your present life which you like very much and to shelve the problem of the children by making it possible to arrive at a compromise avoiding the stark necessity of a decision if the time had come for one. Perhaps you don't realize that consciously, but it is so. Please be sure that I shall never willingly permit the children to be educated in America.*

Paddy's veil lifts. We see her behind his words. She accuses him of "alleged injustice to Americans." He is forced to revisit his original decision:

First of all any question of how I bring myself to criticise the Yanks
after sending you and the children there is beside the point; I sent you
there to be safe (a) from bombs (b) from the Nazis because I had good
reason to believe that England was due for a visit from both; and I
knew that you wouldn't get bombs in the USA and the Americans at
their worst were still democrats and believe in freedom. We got (a)
but not (b) owing to the work of the RAF, the Army, the Navy, the
British people and the Red Army. If you think I had any other reason
have a look at photographs of bombed British cities and (if you caught
hold of any) some of the photographs of Nazi atrocities published by
the Soviet or Polish governments.

He feels compelled to say some nice things about America, but he doesn't
stay with it long. The friendly, generous and kindly people, the lovely
country, soon vanish. He takes that picture down from the wall. He
hangs up another representation of America. He claims that it is back-
ward, socially and politically. The friendly people, the average Americans,
are abysmally ignorant, "which is why I don't want the children educated
there." They are mentally lazy. Their ignorance leads them to engage in
"Jew baiting, Negro baiting, Red baiting." He condescends to say that
America is the youngest nation and still has a lot to learn. All in all, however, he does admire America. He condescends to say that the "Yanks" are
learning fast, using European experience to their benefit. He admonishes
her not to judge America by the few people she has met. He has met millions of Americans in books, poems, music and the cinema. Therefore,
he knows more than she does.

I soon tire of this back-and-forth between them on the virtues and sins of
America. Like me, Paddy seems to have had enough. She asks for a change
of subject. He responds:

So you want "everyday news". Im sorry my dear, I would like to give it
you but I don't live an everyday life – very few of us do – to that extent
anyway. I cant tell you about my work any more than you can me about

yours: and since it occupies me from 9 a.m. till 10, 11 and 12 every night there isn't much left is there?

I manage to get to the flicks now and again but thats about all. I see Esther during my work sometimes and if I finish at a reasonable time we sometimes have supper together. That is about the extent of my relaxation.

I miss the children very badly: but most of the time I realize, that there are plenty of children over here, and I can put the fact that I have some of my own into a separate compartment together with the other things I used to have of my own in the days before the war.

He is still our father but he is lost to us. Our mother tries to maintain the bond. She sends us across the sea in pictures and gramophone records. He responds with delight:

Next the gramophone records. They are grand especially the third and fourth sides. I especially liked Peter's speculation about the cow that "got moved away" and the description of the melon. Am I right in surmising that he tends to lead and Felicity to follow: Also Felicity's description of the fight and her soldiers in the Black Watch (Im getting better at understanding them!) And tell Felicity that Grandma Vaughan says she has seen lots of watermelons as big as a pig! It will be really nice to see a water melon again after that – perhaps almost as nice as to see all of you – though not quite.

Paddy, on her side, must have had her own compartment of things she had before the war. And there she stored him. Somehow she failed to open that door for us. I am sure I never asked about him nor do I remember being told about him. By now, I am nearly six years old. He no longer figures in my life nor in my memories.

Money enters their conversation more frequently. He claims not to be concerned about her spending. His only permanent worry is our education. He wonders if we can read yet. How is our writing getting on? If we are too long in an American school it will be very hard to catch up with English children

Two months pass until we hear from him again. On December 18th, he writes his last letter of 1943. She has written him twice. He apologizes for his silence. He has, without warning, been transferred to Birmingham, "the biggest HOLE in the world." He only gets home on weekends.

He takes up the money question with a new seriousness and sense of urgency:

> *Now I think it is time we got down to the some brass tacks on the money question. I wouldn't attempt to dictate to you how you should live; what I have tried to point out is what you pointed out to me with regard to my little dream (I can hardly think of if as anything else now) of coming out to the States myself after the war; that money earned in England doesn't get you very far in the USA. Quite frankly I don't see how we can go on on the present arrangement. When I started sending you money I had just cleared off the debts I incurred over your passage out; I had no reserves. Since then I have on the average had a running balance of 40 to 20 pounds at the bank. Never any more...I cant see where the most impor-tant item of all is going to come from and that's your passage back home.*

The future is staring them smack in the face. He has been talking around. He has spoken to some U.S. soldiers, even some from Minneapolis, "who tell me that $125 per month is a shop assistant's wage":

> *If the British Consulate is too damn mean to pay you any more (I know what I'd say to a 5 shilling a week raise if I was really in a hole) surely there are American firms who pay wages based on American standards of living?*

He misses the point. If she were a man, she would be paid more. This she always knew.

After much discussion and more elaboration on the financial picture, he says he can continue to send her 16 pounds a month:

But this must be conditional on our making definite plans <u>now</u> about your coming home. You say that theres a six months waiting list for passages; that's six months for us to work out ways and means. And, while on this subject isn't there some scheme of assisted or even free passages? Youre in a better position to find out than me but I shall make enquiries at this end too.

The question as to when and how we shall come home has occupied his mind for several months. Now, however, he believes a decision is imminent:

Ive decided on balance, against up to now because of the dangers of the passage home and the wrench it would be for the children. But the end of the war is approaching – as far as Germany is concerned this year should see it out – and if we wait till then, we'll wait too long. But the overriding fact is the impossibility of carrying on as we are at present. Put it this way. Shall we set a target date – say next May or June – and bust ourselves to save every penny we can to buy tickets then? I think if we worked along those lines we wouldn't find it so difficult as it looks now. Anyway, until I hear from you I shall act as though that's what we're going to do and by the time I get your answer I shall know whether its at all possible from my end anyway.

The year 1944 begins in less than three weeks. We are still wrapped up in this war game. It is fast changing and we are trying to keep up.

CHAPTER 19

1944

TOM WRITES HIS FIRST LETTER of the year on March 12th. He hasn't heard
from Paddy for nearly three months. But she has written to her mother, a
letter dated December 19, 1943, which she has saved in carbon copy. Her
mother, whom he calls "Mum," shares the letter with him. He expresses his
concern:

> It seems to me that something about the USA doesn't at all agree with you;
> or else (which comes to the same thing) you have got into a thoroughly
> run-down condition and need a real rest – mental as well as physical.
> Just how much chance there is of that you know better than I do, but what
> has happened makes me feel all the more certainly that you must come
> home and quickly too. What happens then depends on a whole number
> of things which we cant profitably discuss right now; but it would give me
> a chance to get you properly vetted without continuous nightmares about
> bills hanging over our heads; and to get the children's education started.
> As I can see it those are the two most important jobs now.

I consider what he does not say, that he misses her and wants her back. Nor
does he profess an enduring love, still alive after years of separation. Rather,
he wants to "vet" her, whatever that may mean. It seems to have something
to do with money or her health. As for us, he does not say he wants to hold
us in his arms or look into our little faces. He wants our education to begin.
He will send us to school, St. George's Harpenden to be exact:

138

I went down a fortnight ago, and it is a lovely place; and the teachers obviously know their job and are <u>really</u> fond of children. I cant talk much about it, but I think you know you can trust my judgment as far as schools are concerned; I am sending the prospectus by sea mail so I hope you will get it this year – that will do more than I can. In any case of course nothing can be settled until you have seen the place and people, but I would just like your agreement for me to enter them – it will only cost 2.2.0 and if anything happens of course it could be dropped. I suggest September 1945.

He thinks perhaps we should go as boarders. "Personally I don't see why not."

We will be not quite eight years old in September 1945. If we do return to England we will have been gone for five years. Would he really send us away again?

I try to imagine what my mother might be thinking. There she is, comfortable in our Portland Avenue duplex, busy with her new job, seeing us off to school in the mornings, nicely dressed and reasonably happy. She can rely on Edith, our live-in helper from the farm, to care for us until she returns from the office. Our lives are settling. We are housed, clothed, fed. We are no longer homeless wanderers. Somehow our mother has brought us here. Now our father wants us back.

He closes with love and kisses for us. He says we are quite old enough to write him letters now and again.

He writes again in early April. He has received her letter of February 29th. She has enclosed a large photograph of herself. She wears a full length dress, a housecoat. The photograph is black and white, but I remember the dark blue velvet. Christine had made it for her. It fits her slender body perfectly. She is well-coiffed and watering some flowers. He is not pleased. He has also read two letters which she sent to her mother. Not only is he not pleased, he is furious:

All the letters were full of evasions of the kind to which I have become accustomed from you. But the procrastinations and shelving of responsibility which were excusable when you were young <u>provided you really</u>

made an attempt to make decisions are no longer excusable now when every action you take intimately affects a number of other people—our children, I myself, and our families, to begin with.

I read on. I am shocked by his outpouring of anger and recriminations. I want to run to my mother's side to defend her. Six pages, twelve sides, a litany of accusations. Even the ink is darker than his usual light grey. As if words were not enough, he must assault her eyes as well. I tell myself I must be fair. I should pull back, read this dispassionately, try to understand him. He has had to keep himself under tight control, a necessity of living in a world at war. But the war is loosening its grip, allowing him to look into the future. He doesn't like what he hears from her and probably hasn't for some time. He drags out the past, her affairs with two of their friends, which he seemed quite happy to accept at the time. He even regarded them as youthful explorations leading to personal growth. Now these affairs become ammunition for his rage:

We were all young it did no ultimate damage to any of us – in fact a lot of good on one condition only: that we learnt from our experiences more about our own strength and weakness and on the basis of what we learnt shaped a policy towards life which would bring into use our strength and buttress our weakness. For a time during the early years of our marriage you made some effort in that direction; and your going to America and being put down on your own two feet with no one to lean on was the test of whether you were going to carry on those efforts.

He seems to have forgotten that her going to America was not voluntary. She did not set herself this test. It was his idea. She did what she had to do, but not in the way he had envisioned:

It is clear now that you have failed. It is clear that you are still trying to live the same sort of life at 30 that you were at 20. The difference is that at 20 you had no responsibilities except to yourself; now you have responsibilities to a least three people – Peter, Felicity and myself – that outweigh your own; and to your family and my family also. I am leaving out of account your responsibility to the millions of men, women and children who are being tortured, starved and killed so that you can wear a nice housecoat and arrange flowers in a vase. This would mean nothing to you or you would not have sent me that photograph.

He continues his attack, becoming even more personal:

The war is a struggle between my sort of people and your sort; between those who would to some extent or other have thought out for themselves what they want out of life and will fight for it; and those who take what's handed to them on a plate.

Does he think that the last four years of her life have been handed to her on a plate? Now that she has safely established herself, he wants to diminish all that she has endured, all that she has done. He even accuses her of dismissing her own family:

It is a struggle in which three of your brothers and your brother in law are in the front line; and your husband and another of your brothers in the support trenches. Any one of us, your mother, father, mother-in-law (our childrens' grandparents) as well as all your relations might at any time be killed in every action in this struggle. You know that is not an exaggeration but simple truth. Yet the most enthusiastic thing you can say is "I would like to see my parents again."

He is hitting her hard. Why now, I wonder? Why so damning and cruel? There may be some truth in what he says. She always lacked a certain sensitivity. Personal vanity was also a part of who she was. Both these qualities are front and center in the infamous housecoat and flowers photograph. But dozens of letters notwithstanding, neither of them can really know the other's life.

He travels his rageful path to its destination, answering my question:

You have at last come out in the open because I have made a straight request, that you should now start making arrangements about coming home. You have made it plain that you do not intend to come back to England at any time because you are far too comfortable in the U.S.A. and prefer the American way of life to the English. About that I do not intend to argue although I could: for you have a perfect right to prefer anything to anything else. However it is my wish, and I believe, yours too that our children should get an English education.

This fury is not only about our education. I sense desperation, a looming fear that he will not get us back. She has the goods and the goods are us. There are thousands of miles between us, rendering him powerless. He fights back:

The question of whether you live in U.S.A. or Timbuctoo has nothing to do with this; our children are English and shall be brought up as Englishmen. The second point is that you are under obligations to me, your husband; do not force me to remind you of them by all the means that are open to me. Both these points are completely ignored in your letter to me. In fact, the three letters, when taken together constitute the expression of a such a shallow, ignorant selfishness that had I not been well inoculated by all that has gone before I would have had a very nasty shock indeed. As it was I was more or less prepared but I am still angry and disappointed; not with you- but with myself and partly with the system we are under which can make such monkeys out of nice human beings.

Is this an apology? How can he say he is not disappointed with her? He accuses her of failing to recognize that her first duty is towards the children. He cannot see that she may in her own way actually be putting us first. She may not want to disrupt our lives further. We may better off in the relatively safe and secure life which is now ours. For us, England is a foreign country. Those we left behind are strangers.

I must rest here for a while. His letter continues at great length and gets no kinder. I take time to consider. Why am I writing this story? Who wants to hear it? I do not claim special circumstances unique to my family, my parents. This is simply our war story. There are thousands of others more compelling, tragic, with irreparable consequences. We are quite ordinary as we struggle with separations, damaged relationships, failures in understanding, uncertain futures.

I write because my parents have given me this gift. The letters have found their way to me. He wrote them. She kept them. I don't know why she did. I do not know why she did not share them with me. Too much exposure for both of them, perhaps. Too much to explain. Too much pain. This letter of April 1944 is very painful. I cannot feel her pain but even now his is palpable. His years of stored anger are in every word, every finely constructed sentence. Do I really want to know this? He seems to hate her. I am brought up short. Until now my journey through his letters have been a wonderful opening into my past. These years of the war have been outside my memory. The letters fill a void, answering questions for me. Who was he? Who were my parents to each other in those days? Where did we, the children, come into the picture? Now, as I read and write, I find I am becoming the child of torn loyalties. Whom to believe, whose side to take? I am in pain. But I am also the writer. I don't get to choose. The writer wins. I must continue.

He is responding to three letters, one from her and the two that her mother has shared with him. Paddy has apparently given reasons for her reluctance to return to England. He demolishes them one by one:

(1) You are a Government servant and therefore cannot make independent plans. This is futility. You are in a job; you can leave that job tomorrow without any difficulty – if you want to.

(2) There is no sign of the war ending. I don't know whether this extraordinary statement came out of your own head or is an extract from one of your political reports. The consistent wrongness of our Foreign Office and Diplomatic Service on all major questions since 1918 points to the latter. The point is of course that it suits you at present very well to believe this because it fits your inclination to postpone and procrastinate.

(3) The children could not get accustomed to English rations. This also is tripe and well you know it. Of course they could. It would be more correct if you said you couldn't. .

(4) You cant get a passage. This is quite correct. I also have made enquiries. As the Lisbon route would cost several hundred pounds it is out...but there is

no reason on earth why you shouldn't put yourself on the waiting list – unless you just don't want to.

As there is no immediate prospect of a passage becoming vacant there is no need for cables etc. in getting this fixed up. You write and tell me you have done it: I am writing now to them confirming and asking for instructions as to the payment of the fares. Perhaps it will be 12 months before you can make it. The time to start making plans is still now.

He adds fuel to his fire. He reminds her that "we" sent the children away to avoid German, not Japanese, bombs. Somehow she has become his partner in the decision to leave. That is not how I heard it from my mother, decades later. She did not want to go. She was not given a choice. She was caught in the rush of panic and fear. She was swept along, passports and us in hand, with quickly packed bags, onto the train at Euston Station, headed for Glasgow and the departing convoy. His admonishments ultimately lose their bite, as he is forced to admit that that there is no prospect of a passage in the foreseeable future.

This is not the end of the things he has to say. He will probably divorce her, but that's not certain at the moment. He knows that she does not want to live with him again. He doesn't want to live with the person she has become. He attacks her effrontery in asking for sympathy from her family. He mocks the "widowed sort of life" she claims she is leading:

You try putting your line over to a group of London housewives some of whose husbands and sons have perhaps been prisoners since Dunkirk and see what they'd say to you.

He is furious with her for suggesting to her parents, both over seventy, that they come to the U.S.A. She fully exposes herself as "an escapist and a wishful thinker" with this proposal. He reminds her that her parents have other children, friends, and have lived in Oxford all their lives. For now, I can side with him here. But in 1947, Paddy arranged passage for her mother on the Queen Mary to New York. She came to Minnesota and spent the summer with us at the St. Croix River. It was very hot that year. I have a photograph of my grandma with us, the twins, sitting in lawn chairs. None of us look very happy.

He is not finished. Her attitude towards his family is next. His brother, Peter, who is in the Navy at Madagascar and the Indian Ocean, has written to her several times. She responded with a Christmas card. Tom tells her that this was insulting. "If you can't be bothered to write to my relations, just let it go."

He moves on to his own mother. He reminds her that she is old and has only two grandchildren, us. It seems that Paddy has offered to send her groceries:

Why do you pretend to consider her at all when you have deliberately ignored her for the past eighteen months?

You see my mother doesn't talk about you and I don't talk to her about you either; but she noticed and was very deeply hurt by the fact that the children said nothing to her on the records you have sent from time to time and are apparently unaware of her existence. This may be a complete misreading of the position – indeed I hope it is – but I would like you to remember that she occupies exactly the same positioning relation to our children as your mother does and deserves exactly the same amount of consideration.

There is plenty of pain to go around. Grandma Vaughan is feeling it too. But on this one I check Paddy's box. Mothers of mothers often come out ahead where grandchildren are concerned. Did Grandma Vaughan ever write to Paddy or to us? It is unlikely. At least there is no evidence that she did.

Finally he seems to be running out of steam. He says this letter is already too long. It is. But it is a watershed moment for whatever might come next. His stream of discontent has bursts its banks. He departs with a final zinger:

You suggest I should sell the house. When I do, it will be with one object – to get ready cash for the children's education and perhaps to help pay for your passages if I can make it out of my earnings. None for me and none for you. Is that understood?

On June 24, 1944, he sends his next letter. The ink in his pen has returned to pale grey. Perhaps he can write with a lighter touch, his hand released from the angry tension of his last letter. He has received two letters from her within a day or two of each other. He is relieved to hear that she will put her name down for a passage home. Now he can settle down and wait confidently. He moves on blithely, casually tossing aside an obstacle that could litter the path of our return:

> *There is only one other point I think that arises that needs to be settled now – or indeed can be settled now. That concerns Esther. As far as I am concerned she is out as a factor in the situation. We are good friends as I have many other good friends. That is all – and that is all its ever going to be.*

Here is my dilemma. I know the future. And knowing the future, I know this to be either an incredible lack of insight on his part or an outright lie. I will let it rest there and continue my story.

He wants to stop the back-and-forth about the relative value of the lives they are each leading:

> *Its plainly useless and only calculated to make matters worse for us to continue the argument as to which of us is living the right or wrong kind of life. That is again something that can only be settled when we meet again.*

What is he thinking? How will their being together settle this question? He is peremptory, dismissive, as he so readily dismissed Esther. Paddy's life really doesn't concern him. The decision is to be made on his turf. He would surely have the advantage. He is sure of his position:

> *I can assure you however that I am far from being the Beethoven-esque supporter of the world's troubles you imagine me to be; and I have not only not lost my ability to enjoy life but increased it to an extent that would astonish you – as it has surprised me occasionally. You see I have found that if you live a useful life and throw everything youve got into*

*a cause you believe in and know to be right you automatically enjoy life.
And I might add that there are quite a lot of us over here and we are far
from believing that we wont get what we want in our lifetime; you see it
happens to be what we're fighting this war for and winning it too by God.*

This is Tom, the Communist, speaking, even though he unwarily brings God
into it. He doesn't actually say so, but his pro Russian views and hence his
pro Soviet views are evident throughout his letters. The soldiers of the Red
Army are his heroes. It is true that they are suffering unimaginable horrors
in their fight against Nazi Germany, that they are dying by the millions. In
these letters, Tom pleads repeatedly for the opening of a Second Front in the
West. He faults his own country for delay and prevarication. He cannot be
blamed for this. He is not alone.

He returns to the subject of our education:

*The last point concerns the children's education and what it implies.
It should be plain to you that I would not consider sending them St.
Georges unless I could afford it. If you set your personal comforts above
the education of your children I am afraid I do not. In any case there
is no point in arguing about it. I am putting their names down for
September 1945.*

We don't know what she said to invite this criticism. It seems he will grab at
any opportunity to get in a dig. He continues:

*Nor is there any need to get into a flat spin over our differences of opinion on
the Americans. To avoid going into detail let me refer you to an article by
(I think) Howard Carter in the April or May "Readers Digest" called "The
American Invasion of Britain." It represents the situation pretty fairly. For
my own part I am careful not to let either of the two following things happen.*

He then proceeds to do exactly what he says he will avoid. He cannot resist the temptation to parade his beliefs. He is an authority on all things
American. He has a two-part creed complete with subheadings:

For my own part I am careful not let [sic] either of the two following things happen :

(1) Let my knowledge of the "American way of life" which I know to be corrupt and completely uncultured (in spite of their very high material standards which I admire) mixed up with either

> *(a) my sincere admiration for their technical achievements*
>
> *(b) their genuine, though at present completely muddled and misdirected, feeling for democracy and equality*
>
> *(c) their undoubted generosity and hospitality*
>
> *(d) their niceness or otherwise as individuals*

(2) Let my personal feelings govern what I say and how I act with many English people who do not understand the setup as clearly as I do and let their anti-Yank prejudices (which believe me, have plenty of grounds) carry them away.

Has his arrogance no bounds? All of this for her? He wields his intellectual heavy club while talking out of both sides of his mouth. He begins by belittling what she has come to value. He then condescends to bits of praise before patting himself on the back for his superior knowledge. I ask myself again why am I here? Why do I have to listen to this claptrap? Back off, I say to myself. I am trying to find who he is. That is all. I have chosen to spend time with him. Judgment is not my job.

He leaves D-Day, June 6th, to the very end of the letter. I am surprised. The Allied invasion of France, the landings at Normandy, happened a mere 18 days before he wrote. Perhaps there was too much American in it for him. He does take time out to rejoice:

Well a great deal has happened since I wrote you last hasn't it. D-Day has been and gone. The glider fleet woke me up that morning. I wish I had got up to have a look at it because it's the sort of sight that only comes once in a lifetime. But I am afraid I only thought like many others that it was just another very big raid. "Wolf" has been cried pretty often. But the difference after D-Day and the marvelous success of the 2nd Front! The country has come to life again!

Incidentally Peter might like to know that his daddy had a personal share in the making of all those Horsa gliders our airborne troops went over in.

He is still the father of a son. He wants to share his life in the things that bind men and boys. Joy has its limits, however:

Everyone over here is going strong. There was of course no "celebration" of D-Day. We don't celebrate such things. It was an essential job which had to be done if we were to have a chance and our children also to live the sort of life want to live: that's all.

Thank the children for their birthday cards to me: I have already written to them myself. I think they write very nicely and its most interesting to see the difference already — Felicity much slower and neater than Peter. That's right isn't it? Kiss them both for me.

We are six and half years old. Our mother has made sure we remember his birthday. But I remember none of this. Somewhere in my childhood, I have closed the door to father knowledge. My loss is hidden in the tangles of my brain.

CHAPTER 20

Another Voice

MY FATHER'S LETTERS LIE HERE in a large rectangular cardboard box, in columns by year, spanning 1940 through 1945. So far I have heard only my father speaking. My mother appears second hand, reflected in his writing. Lilian Dubber, my grandmother, now appears, interrupting the flow of my father's words with her own conversation. Paddy saved two of her letters, dated July 29th and August 4th, 1944. They lie resting between Tom's letters of June 24th and September 17th.

Grandma Dubber writes on paper slightly heavier than the wartime airmail my father used. Her return address is embossed in the upper right hand corner: "Homelands, 4 Horspath Rd, Cowley, Oxford, England." I remember this address from my childhood. It is very familiar. I like its rhythm. It has a beat, especially the "Cowley, Oxford, England" part.

Lilian Dubber was a working class woman, a seamstress. Her husband, my grandfather Albert, was a grocer's assistant. She was the mother of six sons and a daughter, also Lilian, whom we know as Paddy, her youngest child. My grandmother was not an educated woman. In spite of this, she writes well. Her style is intimate, mother to daughter. Her script is large and flowing. Her tone is conversational, comfortable, honest.

Her first letter is dated July 29, 1944. She speaks to us:

My dears, Lily, Peter, & Felicity,
    I have been looking for your last letter to answer it, but think I must have sent it to one of the boys, and have not had it returned. However, I

will try and tell you all the news. I was very thrilled when Tom came in to see me on Monday, to tell me that he had seen Mr. Lamb. [Leo Lamb, British Consul visiting from St. Paul] I was sorry that I did not see him too, but as Tom only had an hour to get ready and to be at the appointed place, he hadn't time to call for me but he told me about the meeting, and what Mr. Lamb said about you and the twins. He certainly thinks a lot of you, and praised your work, and naturally does not want to lose you. He also told Tom that he has got two lovely little "brats" over there.

She expresses her concern about Paddy's health, her ulcer, her suffering. She is happy to learn that she is better and putting on weight. She gives motherly advice:

Now dear <u>please do take more care of yourself</u>; don't forget you have a long journey to face, and will want all your strength. Mr Lamb thought probably you would be able to come home next April. Please let me remind again, to take care of everything you have got, pack it all up, and send it on, all household goods are unobtainable here, and you wont find things a No. 7 just the same as when you left there.

There is family news. Hazel, wife of Paddy's brother Fred, is thrilled with the frocks Paddy has sent. They fit her well and she looks very nice in them. Her son Arthur's wife, Mick, is living in London alone. Arthur is with the British Army in India. German bombs have blasted their house for the third time. She writes that Mick would probably be dead if she had not been at work. She signs the letter "I am your loving mother."

Her subsequent letter of August 4th is very different. She responds to a request from Paddy who has asked her advice:

Thanking you for your lovely letter, will answer it per return of post. I am not surprised at the way you speak about Tom. I have noticed for a <u>very</u> long time that he has not been so interested in you and the children. At one time he used to come in and show me parts of your letters, and was

*always so thrilled with the little drawings the twins sent to him, but now
I seldom see him.*

She mentions Esther, though not by name, referring to her as the woman
"staying at No. 7."   This was our house in Lyndworth Close where we had
lived as a family.   Tom is renting two rooms to Esther.   Paddy's brother, Len,
and his family have the rest of the house.   My grandma has a reliable source
for what she is about to reveal:

> *I don't know what influence that Jew woman has over him. They are
> always together, when Tom went to London to work, its funny that she
> should go there too and get a job.   Tom brings her home weekends, and
> they spend practically the whole time together, they eat, go out, and Tom
> spends hours in her room, after their <u>many</u> friends are gone, they are
> alone for hours quite late, which doesn't sound too good to me.   I have
> never seen the woman and I have no wish to do so. After something I was
> told, I had a talk with Tom.   I said I hoped there was nothing between
> them, as they were always so much together, he then said that she was in-
> terested in the same politics as himself and was a help to him, and I must
> trust him, the same as I trust my daughter.*

I want to apologize for my grandma's anti Semitism.   The word stays.   She
was simply a woman of her times and her class.   I cannot edit her.

I am touched by her willingness to confront Tom.   She does not want
to operate behind his back.   Did she really believe this his relationship with
Esther was merely political?   I doubt it.   But she wanted to give him the benefit of the doubt.   She expresses her reservations:

> *I should not be writing to you like this, only that you asked my advice.
> You know that I never like to make mischief between man & wife, so
> please don't think too badly of me.*

She continues with her other concerns:

Now I will go on again. Tom has said one or two things which I have not liked at all. When I approached him about bringing you home, he said that he had no money, and the government would have to do the necessary. When I asked him if there was anything between you, he said well Mum, 4 years is a long time to be parted and you cant expect to feel the same.

He also said that he must wait till you come home to talk things over, and if you don't fall in with his views, you must each go your own ways. This doesn't sound like a happy re-union to me, but of course I may be wrong.

I don't like the thought of you coming back to be unhappy, and to leave such a nice house, and so many good friends, after all if Tom has changed, there is not a lot to come here for. As much as we are longing for your return, don't let <u>me</u> stand in your light, your happiness comes first, who knows we may be able to visit each other after the war.

Eventually I did come to know my grandma. I can hear her well. I can see her in my mind's eye, in her house on Horspath Road, her blunt-nibbed pen in hand as she writes. She is managing this particular loss, but she has had others. A son to suicide, a husband to alcoholism, other sons whom she could also lose before the war is out. She keeps the home. She is a constant in the lives of her family. She is there.

I leave my grandmother and return to what is left of my father's letters. There are very few. He writes on September 17, 1944. His previous letter was in June, just after D-Day. Leo Lamb, British Consul in St. Paul, has somehow managed a transatlantic journey:

Some weeks ago I had the surprise of my life when I got a note from Mr. Lamb. Naturally I lost no time in seeing him. I expect he has already told you about our interview. I was disappointed to learn from him that you had not put your name down for a passage especially after you told me you would: I hope you have now because in any event I am making all my plans now on the basis that you will be coming back next April or May. That is such plans as are possible under existing circumstances.

I, too, am surprised that Consul Lamb has turned up. How did he travel from St. Paul to London in July, 1944? The war is still on. The waters of the Atlantic are alive with U-Boats. I have no answer to this mystery. I summon a fantasy. He opens his office window on the sixteenth floor of the First National Bank Building in St. Paul. He spreads his wings, takes off with ease and speed, to fly across the warring world below, to land in Whitehall, or wherever British diplomats go when they return to home turf. Not so easy for our little family, however, as Tom and Paddy wrangle about when and if we will return. Tom lays down the law. Paddy hesitates to make a move. In addition, the scarcity of passages overlays their personal difficulties. So far, we are going nowhere.

Tom returns to America bashing. This time it is our report cards from school which Paddy has sent him:

I am returning the childrens' reports with this letter. Naturally I am glad to see they are making good progress. I never expected them to do anything else for they are intelligent healthy children — but quite frankly I think the reports themselves are pretentious rubbish. I much prefer the English kind which may not be dressed up in such scientific language but at least tell you something about your children what theyre good at or interested in and how much theyre learning. I wonder by the way whether theyre learning anything? I only ask that because my observation on the Yanks over here leads me to that conclusion.

I want to accuse him of "pretentious rubbish" because he is pretentious and this is rubbish. He can't hear me, of course. I am free to attack.

In spite of all this, he is a good reporter of the current state of war. He is staying in London now. The city has been under siege by German V-1 rockets. The first one was launched immediately after D-Day on June 13, 1944. Thousands more were launched from the French and Dutch coasts against southeast England. The attacks only halted when the sites were overrun by the Allied forces in October, 1944. Over 5,000 Londoners had been killed. Tom was there:

> *Perhaps the most unpleasant part was the driving. As you know I am in the car most of the day and in a car you cant hear anything — not even the sirens sometimes. You just have to watch the people on the street — if you see them looking up and running for cover you know its time to put out the anchors and take a dive yourself. Ive had to do that a few times. Once I jumped out just in time to see one exactly overhead about 100 feet up nearly at the end of its glide, just wobbling in the air. When they are like that they may go anywhere — either straight on or peel off to the left or right and drop straight on you. On this occasion I was about 59 yards from a surface shelter. I think I covered that 59 yards in under 5 seconds. The doodlebug went straight on and dropped about 200 yards away.*

He returns to the invasion, expressing praise and wonder. For now he is in love with the USA:

> *Did you expect things to break up as quickly as they have done? I wouldn't be surprised if you didn't because, although I have always said they would, still the completeness of it took even me by surprise — almost like a dream coming true. I bet they are pleased in the USA with the way their boys are doing. We are over here make no mistake about that... The Yanks have done plenty to be proud of and to put mankind in their debt without trying to minimize our share in it.*

He thanks Paddy for the parcel of clothes she has sent. He admits they came in very handy; but he is not pleased with the quality in relation to their price. He finds the socks useful but too short. He is surprised because US uniforms and accessories "are of marvelous quality." "In fact I should say almost unnecessarily good." Even in this small, petty and foolish way he must undermine her good intentions. He has the last word on everything. I am no longer surprised. I am getting to know him.

We have sent him postcards from our summer camp. He hears that we are enjoying ourselves and wants to know more about it. I remember Sophie Wirth camp. Did I tell him about my solo performance, singing "Paper Doll" at our little camp show? Or perhaps I told him that we sang the national anthem, "O Say Can You See In The Donzerleelight," finishing up with "The Home of the Brain." That is how it sounded to me. I am sure I sang it with great enthusiasm. I love to sing. What did I tell him? All this saving of letters but none from the little scribes. Before ending, Tom pushes Paddy again to put her name down for a passage.

He next writes in November, 1944. He has not heard from her for three months. He sets his condition. He will write no further until he knows that she has booked passage. He accuses her of solving her problems in her own way, shelving them.

> *Since you could not at the last continue to shelve it and continue to write to me at the same time, you stopped writing. This is without any consideration of my feelings. I at least want to know what is happening to my own children.*

I want to give him the benefit of the doubt. He has feelings but what might they be? He may feel abandoned, though he was the one who sent us way. The enormity of his loss emerges as the war subsides. But he makes no effort to spare her feelings. In fact, quite the opposite. He attacks her in small and large ways at every opportunity. He lapses into angry self-pity with a rather peculiar claim that he has ceased to mean anything to her "beyond a background and a meal ticket."

There are occasional tender moments here. He reminisces about the short happy years of their marriage, before the war. But he moves on, summing her up. He says knows her motives very well:

> *You have decided that you would like to stay in the U.S.A keep the children and be free of me. At the same time you want to keep me on a string because I represent certain things, you want to keep up your "Englishness"*

and you want the children to have an English education (represented by the Dragon School). These are all incompatibles and you know it if you descended for a few moments from your cloud cuckoo land to the world of hard reality.

He repeats his demand that she answer "the given question," Yes or No. Will she book passage?

You can cable it if you like; it will save time.

CHAPTER 21
Paddy Joins In

PADDY DOESN'T CABLE. SHE WRITES, her voice strong and clear. On December 5, 1944, with a new year just around the corner, she slips three sheets into her typewriter, two lightweight pieces with a carbon between. She saves the carbon copy, as she did with most of her letters:

> *Dear Tom,*
>
> *I have your letter of November 13th — it arrived three or four days ago since when I have been giving our problem a good deal of thought. Obviously it is impossible for me to say yes or no at this stage — there are too many things I want to know first. But before I start on all that I think I will make a few observations on your letter — No, on second thoughts perhaps I had better weave the whole lot together.*

Weave she does. She takes him apart piece by piece, litigating like an expert:

> *You say that you want me to return to England in order to thrash out our affairs and our future, but, Tom, don't you see that I have absolutely nothing to return to England for except my family and that if we find that we are utterly incompatible (I mean you and I) and we decide to each go our own way what do I have left? I know quite well that you wouldn't help me to return to America and I certainly wouldn't leave the children behind even if I did eventually manage to come back here. In view of all this it seems that I have a right to*

know what to expect should I decide to return in order to try to make a go of our married life.

She takes on his political life. Would he remain active? Would she be left alone night after night as he goes to meetings?

Should the answer to these two questions be 'yes' —am I supposed to like all this, especially with the knowledge that you are being thrown together with Esther.

She blows his cover and reveals what she knows:

I realize that you haven't be [sic] quite honest about your relationship with her. I know that you spend all your spare time with her —that when she was in Oxford you were alone in her room until all hours of the morning — that when your job kept you in London so much she also moved to London — that you drive home to Oxford every weekend together and spend the time there with her. In light of all this I presume that you are living with her in London during the week. Well, if that's what you want it's all right with me, but I just cannot conceive how you expect me to me to fit into such a picture — and why you should ever want me to return. Of course, I realize that it isn't me you want but the children — a fact which doesn't inspire me to return.

She moves on to the next point, making her case efficiently and directly. She challenges him:

You say "Until you do one of the two I can obviously not know what my own attitude is to be" — surely you cannot mean that at this point you don't realize what your attitude is. Surely you must know what you want and what you feel about the situation. You have become so hypercritical of me and despise me so completely that I cannot believe you really want any part of me. You accuse me of shelving my responsibilities: - if only you knew!

She is not asking for pity. She is simply making a bald statement of the facts as she sees them. She is not, however, without a tender line to throw:

> *And I don't mind telling you that if I felt that you were the same person I left behind in 1940 – if I could be sure of your love and affection and co-operation – there is nothing I would like better than to come back to you with the children and say "Here we are, now you take over." There are times when that I feel so tired and lonely that I would love to just give up the fight and be taken care of – but I see no such haven on the horizon.*

She admits that she has been "unforgivably slack" in keeping him informed about us, the children. She apologizes and gives him a brief update:

> *You don't have to worry about Peter's education at this point – I have managed to get him into the best prep school in St. Paul – called the St. Paul Academy, which is run by one John DeQuedville Briggs on English lines. He is very happy at this school and it appears to be doing a lot for him already. They have report cards every month and last month Peter had all A's and B's. Felicity has fully recovered from her operation and is as well and robust as ever, and she is very proud of her 3 ¼ inch scar. She is a very bright and mature child and very much easier to manage than Peter who is sensitive and temperamental, but very appealing and intense.*

I had an emergency appendectomy when I was seven. I was wrapped in a blanket and carried into a snowy night in the arms of a taxi driver. He took my mother and me to St. Joseph's Hospital. In surgery, they placed an ether mask on my face. I heard my own cries become increasingly faint as I lost consciousness. Of course, I survived. I found life in the hospital rather pleasant. Push a button and a nurse comes. She will even pick up the crayon that has fallen to the floor. My surgeon brings me pheasant for lunch as it is Thanksgiving. I don't like it but I keep that to myself.

In this letter, Paddy allows herself a few more tender moments:

Yes, I admit that we were quite happy during those brief years of our married life – and I have never forgotten that you were a wonderful husband in every way and a grand father.

But she is never far from reality:

But that was so long ago and we have both changed so much and frankly I don't believe that either of us would be content to return to such a set-up – we have matured so that we expect more from life. For myself I think I would go quite crazy if I had to stay at home and merely keep house, and what chances would there be for me to get an interesting well paid job in England after the war? You have something which you believe in enough to work and fight for – you have the courage of you convictions – you are an idealist and so are able to feel these things intensely. But I am made differently and I rarely have such strong convictions because I can always see the other side of the question and feel equally sympathetic or unsympathetic towards both sides.

She continues to respond to his criticisms and demands, again litigating in her own defense:

You say that you understand my motives very well, in a way which would suggest that you had figured it all out alone – but you mention all the things that I have told you myself months ago – I admit that I would prefer to live in the United States – obviously I want the children....

She lets go of any tenderness in her next challenge. She even mocks him:

...and at the time that you wrote and said that you didn't know if you wanted me or Esther and that we must fight it out between ourselves – I wrote and told you that I certainly wanted no part of you if you yourself didn't know who you preferred and I certainly wasn't going to try to keep you under such conditions. I must dig that letter out – it was superb!

She levels him further:

> *And as for you having anything to do with my "Englishness" well honestly, don't you agree that that was an incredibly stupid thing to say. I happen to be far more English than you and I cannot see how you have anything to do with my "Englishness" as you call it.*

She is calling out his suspiciously Anglo-Indian mother, Granny Vaughan, maker of hot curries, born in Lahore, brought to England from India by her husband, my thoroughly English grandfather, in 1914. They brought their three year old son, my father, with them.

She hits her stride, further deflating his claims:

> *And as for providing me with a background and meal ticket — I'm not quite sure what sort of background you mean — but whatever it is I am sure I can carry on without it as I have not been in the least conscious of its presence. The meal ticket, as you call it, is for the children and not for me! I could live very well on what I earn if I were the only one to support.*

In his previous letter, Tom had chastised her for sending worrying letters to her mother. According to him, both mothers --his and hers --are upset. He tells her that she has gone through life putting her responsibilities on other peoples' shoulders.

Paddy takes him on again:

> *As for my letters to my mother and the worry they cause — I would inform you that Mummy was the first one to start asking questions, these being prompted by your relationship with Esther, your fewer visits to my home and the lessening of your interest in me and the children, and various most untactful remarks and answers you have made to Mummy.*

She may be shading the truth a bit. As far as we know from her mother's letters, Grandma Dubber was responding to Paddy's request for information. Be that as it may, Paddy uses the opportunity to expose him again:

If your love life had to blossom forth in the way it has I wish you could have exercised a little more discretion and not operated right under the noses of my family. It was entirely unncessary [sic] for you to move her [Esther] to No.7 and insist that she actually share a house with my brother- where he couldn't help but witness more than he wanted to - not to mention your mother and all the neighbours. If you had kept her out of sight they need never have known about her following you up to London.

She throws off the blanket of blame that he has laid on her and lays it firmly back on his shoulders:

Naturally all this is fine if you have decided that you don't want me to return — but it makes things a little awkward since you are still supposed to be married to me. But all that is your affair — except that I do blame you for creating worries for my parents and then trying to make me responsible for them. If I choose to confide in my mother I have every right to do so — she was the first one to start the subject and it would have been useless for me to ignore her questions — she would have worried just the same. But had you been more discreet she would have had nothing to worry about.

She has a chance to speak her mind. She does it. She sums up with a clear statement of their shared reality:

All this doesn't seem to be getting us anywhere — I hate the idea of a divorce just as much as you do — but perhaps we are simply victims of our conditioning and it would be 'bigger minded' of us to admit that our marriage is a failure on the grounds that we have been separated over a period of so many years that we have developed along different lines and are, therefore, no longer compatible.

In her final paragraph she completes her task. She takes what he has had to offer and turns it back. She applies the coup de grace, gently, deftly:

If you still feel that we should see each other (I certainly do) – then I would suggest that you make the necessary plans to visit us as soon as you are able. There are possibilities that I might get a much better job in the not too distant future and should this be the case I may be able to help you with your expenses if necessary. But I am not daring to count on the job at this point in case the whole thing is a flop.

He is rapidly losing the upper hand.

She writes again on December 13, 1944, the day after our birthday:

The children received your telegram – it was phoned to them yesterday and the actual cable was received through the mail today – they will be writing to thank you.

She continues with bits of news. Our birthday party that had to be quickly rearranged because Peter broke out with the chicken pox. The helpfulness of neighbors. The yellow quarantine card on our outside door. The invitation for lunch on Christmas Day at the home of Consul Lamb:

Naturally I cannot accept the invitation definitely at this point as I feel sure that Felicity will be down with chickenpox by then – even if I'm not. We are certainly through a lot of trouble over here – first their tonsils, then German measles, next real measles, followed by appendicitis, and now chickenpox – not to mention my ear, ulcer, throat ulcer, and strep throat.

More news. Bud has taken her to see Paul Robeson in <u>Othello.</u>

Oh, Tom, it was a wonderful performance and I don't think I have ever enjoyed anything more. I wish so much that you could have seen it – had you done so I think you would never want to see Othello himself played by a white man.

I stop in my tracks. Many years later in London I saw a white man play Othello. My father was in blackface in a performance by his own small company, The Unity Theater. She was right. It didn't work at all.

Bud is now more than a walk-on in our drama. He is full stage, front and center. Paddy envisions a scene where Bud and Tom sit down together in great congeniality with her as admiring audience:

> *I would so love to get you and Bud together and listen to you talk about the affairs of the world. He is extremely well informed on all subjects — and is fair and very pro-British though I don't think he much cares for English people — except as individuals.*

She lets her guard down, just long enough for a few moments of longing:

> *Oh Tom, I wish so much that we could be together again- not as we were, but living a fuller life in the light of our experiences of the past four and a half years. Do you suppose that you could ever love me again? Both last year and this I was very touched by the simple phrase in your birthday cables to the children "Kiss Mummy for me" — how much did that mean?*

> *Darling, I hope that you are happy, but I wish so much that you were here to share the children with me — they are getting so interesting now and you could help them so much — and the older they get the more they will need you and from my point of view I know I would enjoy them even more if I could witness your interest and pleasure in them.*

> *Good night, Your wife.*

Paddy saved letters; but she also saved a curious exchange of memoranda between His Majesty's Consul in St. Paul-Minneapolis and The British Under Secretary of State for Foreign Affairs, dated January 19, 1945. Through lawyers Messrs. Adler and Maurice Cohen, Tom has been making inquiries regarding the return to the United Kingdom of his wife, Mrs. Lilian Vaughan. These inquiries made their way to the desk of British Consul Leo Lamb who replies to the Under Secretary, presumably to be passed on to the lawyers:

Mrs. Vaughan states that she has been in correspondence with her husband on the subject of her return and wrote to him at some length about a month ago.

He should therefore now be in possession of the letter in question.

He also states he met with Mr. Vaughan in Oxford in July:

He asked me on this occasion to assist his wife and children to obtain a passage home when the time came for their return. This I am, of course always willing to do, though the allocation of passages depends upon the facilities at the disposal of the Ministry of War Transport. The decision as to when to undertake the journey is, however, a personal one between Mr. and Mrs. Vaughan.

It is not sufficient for Tom to press Paddy for her answer. He is exploring legal options, not stated, though probably related to future decisions regarding custody of the children. Leo Lamb continues his letter to the Under Secretary, addressing practical concerns:

I would at the same time observe in this connection that whereas last autumn there were reasonable grounds for expecting that the dangers from enemy aerial attack might be terminated in the comparatively near future, the continuation of attacks by Robot bombs and the subsequent appearance of the V.2 missiles, in conjunction with the recent reverses on the Western Front, would seem to indicate the necessity for a revision of the expectation of such an imminent to more normal conditions. The final decision in such matters must in any case in my opinion, as already stated, rest with the individuals concerned according to the circumstances of their particular case.

The matter seems to end there. But Tom has tried this new arrow in his quiver. At the moment it doesn't seem to be very useful as a way of exerting pressure on Paddy.

Half a year passes. In late May, 1945, Paddy sends a short note saying that she hasn't heard from him since November. She underlines the month for emphasis. She writes that we are all very well and happy. We, the children, are growing. We spend the weekends at the St. Croix River. Life is good. She would like to hear about his life, what he is doing now in his "work and personal affairs." She understands that he has sold their house and asks if he has received a good price for it. She asks what has he done with the furniture. Her words come from a great distance, of time, of place, of relationship. She might not be surprised if she never hears from him again.

But she does, in a most unexpected way. He sends a cable dated June 6, 1945. The yellow paper lies, fragile, between my fingers. Edges ragged. Text brief.

Message terse. "ARRANGING TICKETS WITH CUNARD LETTER FOLLOWS. TOM VAUGHAN."

I do not understand. Are the tickets for her and us? Or are they for only him in response to her December suggestion that he come for a visit? This is unlikely. "Tickets" are plural. They must be for us. She has not yet told him yes or no. Maybe he can force an answer from her. The message is peremptory. It has a "take it or leave it" quality. Tickets in the works, full stop. Strip away all the back-and-forth, to-and-fro, that has been going on between them. He doesn't particularly want her. He wants us. He cannot quite believe that he may actually be losing us.

CHAPTER 22

Final Words

A COUPLE OF WEEKS LATER his promised letter follows. It clarifies nothing. He does not mention the cable. This is the last letter of his in my possession. He begins with ordinary chat. He thanks Paddy for her letters of December 5 and 13 of the previous year, as well as for Peter's report and school prospectus. He will write to us children under separate cover. We must have written him at times for he is impressed with our spelling and handwriting. Over the years and the miles between us, he has managed to hold us in his mind:

> *Peter is interested in the way things work – OK I always knew that right from the time he used to shove pebbles down the drain, and he is physically clever – I can see that from the latest cinema film – but I would much rather see him become a surgeon or a physicist or something of that kind than an engineer – and he is just as likely to. Felicity is different; she might become anything. She certainly knows how to put a letter together.*

Peter and I are nearly eight years old. I remember many things from my life then. My home, my school, my friends, my new family. But I have no memory of my father, much less writing and receiving letters. His very existence was outside my awareness. I remember him only as a subject that never came up.

He makes a final declaration, his once-and-for all moment, his final ending:

Now to deal with the main portion of your letter. I am going to be quite blunt.

If this cross-talk about whether I want you or whether I don't and what is going to happen if I don't is starting another lease of life I see no object in our resuming our correspondence. I have put the things which I feel in my last letter and I don't propose to repeat them. Whether I shall be happy or not is one thing and whether you will be happy or not is another, but what is the crux of everything is whether we are – both of us – to recognize our obligations to one another and to our children. I am making no conditions and I never have; I am asking you as I have been asking you for eighteen months now to come home. Either say yes or no so that we know where we stand. I am making no promises because it would be grossly unfair to everyone concerned if I did. Nor do I expect you to. That is all. If you answer this letter please say yes or no – that is all that is necessary now.

He gets that out of the way, as in an unpleasant task completed. He drops back to casual chat. He thinks she will be interested to know that he has no grey hairs yet though he is now 34 years old. He is busy with work and elections. He takes a swipe at Peter's report card and the American educational system. Two full pages of that. He states he will not be at ease until we are at St. Georges or a similar "good" English school. He still holds us in his future. Paddy does not get similar welcoming treatment:

To conclude. You seem amazed that I am not prepared to throw myself enthusiastically around your neck when you eventually get round to doing something I have been asking you to do for a year and a half. You seem to think one can just chop five years out of one's life like cutting a piece of cake. I have many faults but intellectual dishonesty is not one of them. Things have happened during those five years which have changed both us and the relationship between us. These are facts which must be recognized and faced up to; if you do not it will be the worse for you later on. I am asking you to help yourself – not me; I can look after myself as I have been doing five years now without your assistance.

So much for her longings, which she dared to express. They are nothing but intellectual dishonesty. He makes a final plea:

> *I am asking you to take a chance – possibly the last chance – of facing your responsibilities with me, fulfilling them and making our marriage in reality what we hoped it would become eight years ago. We cannot pick up where we left off in 1940. Too much has happened. In some ways it will be worse in some ways better but it will all the time be different. And I might add that we shall have a much better chance of making a go of it if you come home voluntarily and are not shot out of the USA when you exit permit expires and the money stops in September.*

He doesn't like her and doesn't trust her. He lectures her as if she were a willful child. He does not know the woman who has created this new life for herself and their children under extreme conditions. He asks her to come home voluntarily. Does he remember that her leaving was not voluntary?

As the writer, I need a few moments to puzzle over my role here. Through the letters of my parents I have become audience to a play in which I played a part. Peter and I are little ghosts in the wings. Paddy and Tom struggle center stage over their relationship, but it is really all about us. I control the narrative now. I want to be fair to them both. Nonetheless, I find myself taking sides -- Paddy's side -for that has been my life. It is difficult for me to stand next to Tom and understand him. His blaming and arrogance offend me. But if I can sense his helplessness, perhaps I can feel compassion for him. For he is helpless where his little ghosts are concerned. He cannot reach us, retrieve us, except through the force of his written words.

He anticipates her return. But he warns her of his limits:

> *So do not expect the old ecstasies. They aren't forthcoming – yet. I have got to get to know you again and you have got to get to know me. Then we may learn to love one another in a new and better way.*

I want you to think these things over carefully and then answer — yes or no. Then I shall know how to act.

He cannot resist a final mean dig:

I must say I never shared your good opinion of Mr. Lamb. I couldn't think of a worse type to represent Britain to the Americans. He even tried to patronize <u>me</u>.

This final paragraph is a low blow. Leo Lamb, British Consul in St. Paul, Minnesota, not only gave Paddy a job. He gave her respect and work that uses her technical and personal skills. We can put aside our wandering life. We have landed and not so far from our British roots after all. Tom has really hit Paddy where she lives.

I turn over the final page to its blank side. But it is not blank at all. It is full of scribbles, little drawings, problems in long division, all rendered in thick black pencil, the kind that Bud brought home from the newspaper. Tom's letter has become scratch paper for both adults and children. I see my hand here in the heads of curly-haired girls, drawn full face and profile. There is a childish outline of a ship at sea with six portholes and steam arising from a funnel. There are two attempts to divide 1888, first by 8, and then by 38. The number 369 is divided by 3. Either Peter or I have practiced writing in large capitals the name of our local railroad, the Soo Line. Where, I wonder, had this letter had been lying that it should receive this kind of attention? Casually tossed down for anyone to read?

Paddy writes a month later. She thanks Tom for this letter:

I thank you for your letter of June 23rd — it was extremely interesting in many ways but you still haven't explained what plans you propose to make for our return. Since there are to be no traces of the "old ecstasies", let's deal with this thing on a strictly business basis. You have not kept me informed of any of your movements with regard to the selling of the house, the condition of our belongings, what I would need to bring in the way of household requirements, where we would live and how – and last but not least, what you propose to do about Esther.

Where shall she send the trunks? What is his income? If we are to go the Dragon School, he will need to pay fees. She will not live with relatives but perhaps one of his mother's apartments is available. We can only bring the clothes we have, for there is no money for new things unless he can send extra funds. Our return tickets must be from St. Paul. She is afraid she will not have money enough to pay for our needs on the journey to New York:

I have only $20 in the bank and the children have about $15 between them in war stamps – that is all. So you see that financially it is going to cost a lot to get us back to England and I have extremely little to contribute. What is your financial position?

She gives him an out, if he wants it. But she is challenging him as well:

Lastly, you don't <u>have to</u> have us back merely because you feel it is your duty and because you think the children will be better off in England. We are all <u>very happy</u> here and the children enjoy a sense of stability and a good environment – which would be even further enhanced if I were able to marry Bud, who loves the children and could do so much for them if he were in a position to do so. As it is he is almost like a father to them and we have much to thank him for. We are giving up a <u>great deal</u> by returning to England and so I want you to realize that we expect you to see that our sacrifice is not in vain. By that I mean that we hope to find you at least half-way human, and couldn't you possibly dig deep and try to unbury your old sense of humour – I'm sure you had one once. Your letters over the past two or three years have been so hard, inhuman and completely lacking even a trace of humour that I find the prospect of meeting you again somewhat of a nightmare.

This opera will not end on a stage full of dead bodies. But the music rises in crescendo. Paddy is on stage, arms flung wide. She actually never could sing a note, except for "God Save The King" (or later, "The Queen"). But I give her voice here as she tells him he cannot tread on her. She is a bit cruel perhaps. But she is honest.

Tom strikes back. I don't see his letter among those she saved. But I have her response in carbon copy, written August 20, 1945:

> *Dear Tom,*
>
> *I was profoundly shocked by your unrestrained and vulgar outburst of August 1st – I would never have believed it possible for you to sink to such a level and the only excuse I can think of is that you have been badly hurt. If that is the case I know it could not have been hurt caused by jealousy as you have long since ceased to care enough – therefore I presume that your pride must have been shaken. But that wouldn't damage anyone.*
>
> *Most of your letter isn't worth comment – it is too utterly absurd – but there are one or two things that I will try to straighten out.*

I take a minute to consider. Where is his mystery letter? What did she do with it? It can't have been an accidental omission. Paddy was scrupulous in saving correspondence. The Pepperidge Farm bag contained an archive of stored relationships. Friends, lovers, family were there for her to touch in her wartime isolation. There are letters from Frank and Lynn and other faceless men who passed through her life in England before the war and now in America. There are dozens from Bernard, who may also have been her lover as well as a friend of Tom and herself. Her brother Arthur wrote from India where he was posted during the war. There are letters from her mother. She saved carbon copies of many letters she wrote from her desk in the British Consulate. A letter to her brother Len. Another to Tom's mother. But Tom's egregious letter of August 1st is nowhere to be found. I am left to wonder. I listen to her:

> *Firstly, I was all prepared to come home and never dreamed you would suddenly turn on me like that. For a very long time now I have tried to*

get you to show that you are still human enough to try to meet me half-way when attempting to rebuild our home and life together – never once have you given me one word of encouragement – never once have you expressed any plans you had for our return – never once have you told me what developments have taken place with Esther. Two and half years ago you told me that you were in love with each other and that when the time came the decision would have to be made between Esther and me which of us was to have you – that I refused to do; saying that unless you yourself knew which one you preferred I would have no part of you. Don't deny it, I still have every letter you have written to me and I have kept copies of my correspondence to you. I still believe that I have a right to know what is the present situation in this respect and just what I would be up against.

Her financial situation is dire. She has only her small salary for support. But she does not want his pity. He cannot be blind to the effects of his actions:

I suppose you realize that you have damaged yourself severely by refusing to assist with the cost of bringing up the children – you have left us without warning with an income of $140 a month which is totally inadequate even to cover my monthly overhead expenses – just how we will make out I don't know – but obviously that means nothing to you. I have not lived above my income – but I have tried to raise the children in their rightful environment and to do for them what any mother would want to do for her children.

His letter was a bitter goodbye kiss. More a bite than a kiss. He has cut her off. But she does get in a good hard kick as he goes out the door:

Finally, the coldness of all your letters, the almost calculated hostility of them and what can only be termed the willful misstatements and misinterpretation of fact would almost appear to constitute a scheme for making me stay over here and to put me in the position to be blamed so that you can take the children away from me. But you have failed – I am still willing to return to you if only you will give me a written assurance that you will make an honest effort to meet me half way in our attempt to rebuild our lives together. If you cannot do this in all sincerity then do your damndest and I will fight every inch of the way to keep the children.

I am surprised that she would throw him this one last little bone, one last chance to salvage their relationship. But there could not be much meat on that bone. It has been pretty well chewed. There is no nourishment in it for either of them.

In her final words, she exposes him:

Perhaps the cheapest remark in your letter was "I shall continue to keep in touch with the children — unless of course you prevent them from receiving my letters" — such a remark hurts nobody but yourself. But don't worry, they won't even be told that you are no longer helping to support them.

Paddy and Tom are finished.

There are no more letters between them. Nor has the Pepperidge Farm bag yielded up any letters from Tom to us children. Would Paddy have saved them if he had written? That page is as blank as my memory of him.

Tom vanishes, but Paddy worries about what he may be doing backstage. She fears that Messrs. Adler and Cohen are there as well, readying documents for a child custody fight. Tom's behavior has not gone unnoticed by members of the extended family. Paddy writes to her mother-in-law on November 16, 1945. She addresses her as, "My dear Mrs. Vaughan":

Mummy [her own mother] also told me how very upset you are about Tom's behavior — and I am truly sorry that things have worked out thus. Naturally he is a great disappointment to everyone and I cannot imagine what has caused him to change so much, he used to be so sweet and gentle and understanding — but to me it seems that he has turned into something quite evil and frightening and I can only assume that

Esther Mizel is the cause of it all — though it seems almost unbeliev-able that any one human being could play such havoc with the soul of another. She must be damnable cunning and forceful. However, as you say Tom was weak enough to fall into her clutches and he must take the consequences. If people are punished in this life for their sins, then I'm afraid he will be in for a lot of hell.

So far I have steered clear of Esther as I tell my story. It is too easy to assign blame to her on the basis of hearsay and faulty memory. I also want to be fair, for she cannot speak for herself. There are no letters from her. Yet Paddy touches on aspects of Esther that I came to know myself in the following years. Esther could be very persistent when she wanted something to happen, as simple as pressing more food on us, more cups of tea, more biscuits, more cheese. All done with good intentions. I stop here. I am running ahead. I return to Paddy's appeal to Tom's mother:

If you, or Aunt Gwenydd, or anyone other than Mrs. Mizel has any in-fluence over him would you please try to make him see the utter selfishness and folly of trying to take the twins from me.

Can't he be made to realize the awful catastrophe it would cause in their young lives to be uprooted from their home — shipped to a strange country (and England would seem very strange to them), placed in a boarding school where they would be so different from the other children due to their having been raised in America, and with no happy home to go to during their vacations.

If we could have all returned to England together and Tom had pro-vided a home for us and had made up his mind that he was going to be the same good father and husband that he was before we left, everything would have been different. I could have been there to help them through the transition stage and it wouldn't have been so difficult for them — but anything else is utterly out of the question.

Has he actually threatened a move for custody? She seems to think so, but I am unsure. Did I miss something in his letters? She continues to press her case:

> *However, I feel that he has absolutely no legal right to them and I am sure no court would grant him custody of them. I have worked hard for them in every way since bringing them from England and I know I have been a good mother to them and have provided them with everything a child needs as a foundation for a happy normal life – they enjoy a sense of security and the atmosphere of their home is a happy one so that they are free from all worries and they are developing as they should. The fact that he no longer helps with their support and has chosen to disappear completely from our lives will be much against him if he tries to contest a divorce suit against him.*

Paddy closes with wishes for a pleasant Christmas. She is concerned about the effect of her letter:

> *Please try not to let all this upset you too much. I will keep in touch with you as long as you wish it and the children shall write to you from time to time –and when I have any decent photographs you shall have copies.*

There is no evidence that any of this ever happened. My Granny Vaughan vanished, trailing an aroma of hot curries as she passed from my life.

Two final yields from the Pepperidge Farm archive are now before me. I could let them go, pack them away again. No one will miss them. Nonetheless, I decide that they have a place in my story. Surely there are still questions. There may be some answers here. I see two official brown envelopes, marked PRIVATE & CONFIDENTIAL each costing 5 shillings, sixpence postage, King George VI, his crown suspended above his head, on the stamps. Return address London, E.C. 29. They were originally sent to our duplex home at 514 Portland Avenue, St. Paul, Minnesota, probably the last address known to the sender. We moved from there in 1947. They were forwarded to our next St. Paul home at 895 Fairmount. They finally reached the recipients at 695 Lincoln, a few blocks away. We had moved there during my high school years.

One envelope is addressed to Mrs. Lilian Stutz, whom we know here as Paddy, my mother. She is now married to Bud Stutz. Enclosed are documents and a cover letter from Adler and Adler, Solicitors, dated 1st June 1953 and sent from their offices at Devonshire Chambers, 146, Bishopsgate, London, E.C.2. The documents cite a petition filed In the High Court of Justice, Probate, Divorce and Admiralty Division. The letter is as follows:

Dear Madam,

We act for Mr. Thomas Hugh Vaughan who has filed a Petition for dissolution of your marriage on the grounds therein stated.

Pursuant to the rules of the Court and by way of service, we enclose herewith:

1. *Copy of our client's Petition dated 19th May 1953*
2. *Form of acknowledgement of Service*
3. *Form of Notice to Appear*
4. *Memorandum and duplicate Appearance.*
5. *Declaration and Admission*
6. *Addressed envelope*
7. *International stamp*

The letter requests that Paddy return a "Form of Service" for which envelope and stamp are provided.

The petition cites the grounds for divorce. Adultery, of course, the only legally viable option for ending a marriage. These were the days of the Co-Respondent, the adulterous partner of the spouse being divorced. The petition cites the date of Tom and Paddy's marriage, the places of cohabitation of the married partners, the birth of two children, named here, and the current addresses of the Petitioner (Tom) and the Respondent (Paddy).

Is it possible that Paddy is divorced from Tom, but Tom is not divorced from Paddy? According to the petition, this is the case:

That, having obtained a decree of dissolution of the said marriage in the State of Minnesota on the 23rd day of April 1947 and having gone through a ceremony of marriage with one Charles Stutz on the 13th day of June 1947 in the State of South Dakota, the Respondent [Paddy] has lived with the said Charles Stutz as his wife and habitually committed adultery with him.

The Petitioner therefore prays that the discretion of This Honourable Court be exercised in his favour and it be decreed:-

(1) That his said marriage be dissolved.
(2) That he may have the custody of his said children Peter Hugh Vaughan and Felicity Ann Vaughan
(3) That he may have such further and other relief as may be just.

There are two obvious questions, the first is how Paddy managed a divorce if she was still married to Tom? There is a family story, one which I have repeated many times to amuse my listeners and titillate them with its scandalous possibilities. When my mother wanted to divorce my father so that she could remarry, she and Bud went to a friend and neighbor for assistance. He was a prominent St. Paul attorney, very learned and ethical. Based on what he knew of the law, he refused to take their case. He is supposed to have suggested that they seek counsel on West 7th Street where, below the bluff, legal matters were handled a little more loosely. Perhaps there may be someone who can overlook complications and arrange it. It is done. Six years later the details of Paddy's marriage to Bud are known to the Court in London. Attorneys Adler and Adler have done their detective work.

The second question is why does Tom wait so long to file for divorce and seek custody of his children? We are now fifteen years old. He hasn't seen us since we were 2. He cut off all our support in 1945. How could he possibly retrieve us from our mother now? As for the divorce itself, Tom may want to marry Esther. I note the name of one Max Adler on his attorneys' letterhead.

I often heard Esther speak of "my brother, Max." Surely Max is helping here. Admittedly, Tom is in a difficult position. He doesn't have a West 7th Street lawyer to do the deed for him.

Did Paddy return the Form of Service? Perhaps. There is no return envelope and no international stamp enclosed. Perhaps she sent them, as instructed by the Court, if she did not intend to answer the charges. Or perhaps she ignored the whole thing. This could have been a very sticky wicket for her, a respectable matron and mother in the employ of His Majesty's Foreign Office, doubly married.

The second official brown envelope is addressed to Charles Stutz, Esq., 514 Portland Avenue, St. Paul 2, Minnesota, U.S.A. It makes the same journey as Paddy's letter across several city blocks to our home at 695 Lincoln Avenue. The cover letter from Adler and Adler, and the list of enclosures are identical to those sent to Paddy. With one exception:

> *Take Notice that in proceedings in the High Court of Justice by Thomas Hugh Vaughan for divorce, it has been alleged that you have committed adultery with Lilian Vaughan otherwise known as Lilian Stutz. A copy of the Petition is delivered with this notice.*

Bud is the named Co-Respondent, the adulterous partner of the adulterous wife. Enclosed is a Form of Acknowledgement that he must return. The envelope for the return is here, though I cannot find the international stamp. I suspect Bud ignored the whole thing, not knowing what else to do.

He and Paddy remained married for fourteen years. Tom married Esther. I don't know when. But they were together from their first meeting in London during the war until her death in the early 1990's.

CHAPTER 23

Resolution

My American life now takes full possession of me. My child's southern accent, which my father heard on recordings Paddy had sent him, has slipped away. Always sensitive to tone and sound, my ear gathers the harsh, nasal cadences of the Midwest. I carry no sense of myself as different from my friends. I have a "stand-in father" which at the time seems sufficient. My mother is charmingly English and thus quite acceptable in the social sphere of our new world. She is not really foreign. Occasionally, I have a small longing for a mother like those of my friends. They don't work "outside the home." They don't have jobs. They are home to make lunch. But I have acquired an aunt and uncle, cousins, and grandparents who take me in as one of their own. Paddy's marriage to Bud initially brings family and stability.

Paddy's job at the Consulate keeps a little bit of Englishness in our lives. Consuls come and go but they and their families are temporary attenuations, small documentary moments. They arrive from former postings, from places with names like "Marrakesh" and "Basra" and "Singapore. " They stay for a while, then depart to similar places. I have little curiosity about their worlds. I am satisfied with my own.

The Atlantic is peaceful now. Convoys of battleships and destroyers running at top speed between England and Nova Scotia are history. German U-Boats no longer lurk along the Florida coast, keeping us from our oil-slicked beach. But we still cannot cross this immense ocean. We cannot interrupt our lives for a return journey. We have school, work, new families, the business of growing up. Peter and I are held firmly in the custody of our mother.

When we are sixteen, she moves to protect us further. So far we have been dependents on her diplomatic passport, but now Paddy plans a trip. She, Bud, Peter, and I drive from St. Paul to Winnipeg, Manitoba. Peter and I must exit the United States and reenter on our own immigration visas. In this way we become resident aliens with permanent status. In five years we will be eligible to become American citizens. We cannot be whisked off to England in the event of our mother's death.

In the spring of 1959, nineteen years after our wartime departure, Paddy finally returns home. It is to be a visit to her family for a month. Peter is a senior at Yale, I am at Radcliffe. Fledglings about to leap from their Ivy League nests. Paddy books passage on the "S.S. United States." It is "The World's Fastest And Most Modern Liner," according to the Passenger List booklet, another saved item in my mother's stash from the past. It sails from New York on Friday, April 24, 1959 to Le Havre and Southampton:

> ### GREETINGS
> *We bid you a hearty welcome on board the UNITED STATES.*
> *It is the aim and endeavor of our Company to maintain on this great American-Flag liner, service and cuisine of the highest standards, and to provide every facility which will add to the pleasure of the voyage. Every officer and every member of the crew is interested in your welfare and will do his utmost to insure your comfort and happiness on board.*
> *We hope you will thoroughly enjoy your crossing!*
> ### UNITED STATES LINES

Her return journey does not begin in haste and fear. There is no hurried train trip to an unknown point of departure, its location protected by wartime secrecy. There is no tearful father left standing at the rail station. On board there is comfort and cuisine and a helpful crew who want her to be happy. The waters of the Atlantic will not yield attacking U-Boats. The liner is fast, a marvel of seafaring excellence. Its speed, however, is not for escape. This is not the "Duchess of York" sailing in convoy in 1940. It is a modern ship operating in a competitive commercial world: Twelve decks, 2000 beds, 1000 crew. The faster, the better, the shorter the passage, beat the competitors, good for business.

Paddy travels Cabin Class. As a British Vice Consul, she is a dignitary. She is seated at the Pursar's table. She finds graciousness for less money than in First Class, but elegance nonetheless. The red, white, and blue passenger list booklet tells us that "Murals and Decorations on the United States have been contributed by American artists. " Dinner is at 6.30 p.m. "Ladies are asked to refrain from wearing shorts and gentlemen are requested to wear a coat or jacket." We are told of "a choice selection of the finest wines obtainable from the oldest and best establishments in Europe and the United States."

There are kennels for pets, a gymnasium for exercise, a swimming pool, a tobacco shop, and valet service. Gowns can be cleaned for $2.50 to $7.00, price depending on the numbers, size, and style of the pleats (Box Pleats or Side Pleats).

There is a library and writing room on the upper deck, as well as a children's playroom. And more. I do not know how she spends her days on board, but it is a very different journey.

Who is to meet her off the boat train at Victoria Station? A brother? Once she reaches London, she gets her hands on a telephone directory. She leafs through the pages where she looks for Tom. Several Thomas Vaughans answer her calls, but they are strangers. She dials once more. She hears his voice, his "dark brown voice," on the other end. She says, "Tom, this is Paddy." Confused, he doesn't understand. She helps him. "Are you the father of Peter and Felicity?" He replies, "Yes, I am!" She replies, "Well, I am the mother!" "Paddy, where are you?" "I am here," she says.

My mother told me this story. I have recounted it often to others. Tom follows with a letter, from Belsize Grove, Hampstead, N.W. 3, his first to her in 14 years. The letter is dated May 5, 1959, sent to her at the home of her brother Perce:

Dear Paddy,

What a surprise to hear your voice on the phone on Saturday! And yet I suppose I expected you and/or the children to turn up sometime. I should be delighted to see you and hear all your news, especially about Felicity's forthcoming marriage and return to Oxford.

I understood you would be with Percy and Gladys [her brother and his wife] till Wednesday. I have an evening class on Wednesday and in any case you said you wouldn't know when you would arrive back; isn't it so? So I suggest we meet on Thursday. If you like I will collect you from Shirley [Percy's town] — more satisfactory than meeting trains — about tea-time and I can drive you here for an evening meal and you can meet Esther.

I take it your husband isn't with you; but if he is we would both like to meet him as well. In other words he is included in this rather clumsy invitation.

Give my kind regards to your family. I hope enough water has flowed under the bridge now for everyone concerned to let bygones by bygones, but shall quite understand if anyone has not. I know I have anyway.

Yours sincerely, Tom.

I have only just seen this letter, one small sheet among all the others of my recent discovery. As I type his words, I hear him speaking. I am sad, but at the same time I feel a small burst of joy. Sad that he is gone, now forever. Joy now in this link of reconnection. I have read dozens of his letters and thousands of his words over the months of my narrative. I have tried to write them into life, lift them from the paper, and somehow bring him to me. At times he has made me angry. I have not loved him. I have become my mother's defender. I may never be able to say that I love him, but I have come to know him. Time twists my meaning. For I came to know him when I was an adult before I knew him when I was a child.

Tom has heard from Paddy that I am to be married and will be living for a time in Oxford. My life has taken some interesting turns, coincidental enough to challenge the very idea of coincidence. An unseen hand is doing healing work, binding up old wounds and reconnecting torn threads of place and relationship.

In 1957, during my sophomore year at college, I meet Townsend, my husband-to-be, in a Chaucer class. He is known as T. We are sitting in the front row, one chair between us. We become inseparable, knowing almost immediately that we will marry. He is also a rower and, by senior year, he is captain of the Harvard Varsity heavyweight crew. He has decided to do graduate work in English and chooses Oxford. Not because of me, for I do not think he was considering my family history. Through a Harvard professor, he has made a connection to Wadham College, Oxford. We will marry in August and travel to England soon after. Meanwhile, his Harvard crew has completed an undefeated season. They are selected to compete on July 4, 1959, for the Grand Challenge Cup at the Henley Royal Regatta. He will go to England before I do.

Paddy's trip is the first thread in our fabric of repair. I know where my father is. I send him a letter. I have just graduated from college. I fear my letter contained the usual platitudes about commencement and beginnings. What do you say to the actor when he reappears on the stage where he has missed many acts? "Where have you been? " Or, "How nice to see you again!" Whatever I said must have been all right. He told me later how delighted he was to receive it. He remembered my opening sentence. "I have wondered for a long time what sort of man my father is."

He thought we would turn up some day. We have. When I read his letter to Paddy, I thought it sounded a bit casual. "Turning up" did not seem to me quite the right choice of words to describe the end of a rupture that was so lengthy and profound. The English, however, are good at making light of heavy things.

Summer flows, as does the Thames at Henley, where T, my future husband, dips his oar in the water with the rest of the Harvard crew. The annual regatta blooms along the both banks of the river. Colorful tents house sleek shells from many countries. Tea is served at teatime on white tablecloths in exclusive clubhouses. Women's dresses may not rise above the knee. Suspicious skirts are measured at the door to assure compliance. Fancy hats are seen everywhere. Men sport college blazers, some the worse for wear--both the men and the blazers. It is a rower's paradise for boats, frumpery, food, and drink.

Tom was once a rower for his Oxford college, Wadham, the same one that T will attend soon. There is no design here, merely another astonishing coincidence. My father has learned of my upcoming marriage. He also knows that his future son-in-law shares his sport at a level of excellence he himself could never have achieved. He comes to Henley from London for the day and finds my rower at the boat tents. He has watched the crew's workout and is impressed, for they were a beautiful boat. My husband meets my father before I do. "What was it like?" I ask him again. He tells me he noticed little similarities of manner, hard to define. "Perhaps it was something in the way he walked," he says. That surprises him and me as well. In those two and a half years of our brief life together, my father has put his stamp on me.

CHAPTER 24

Reunion

TOM IS FOUND. IT IS time for the last act. Now I can tell those who ask about my writing, "I've almost finished. I can see the end from here," as if it were a place just down the road and around a short bend. But I have done nothing this summer, written nothing. I have taken a vacation from my memoir. I have nursed a deteriorating hip and have scheduled surgery. My husband and I have traveled by car to visit friends at the seaside. We have driven the New York State Thruway and shown up at the annual lakeside gathering of my husband's extended family. I have flown to Minnesota, moving at speed through airports in wheelchairs pushed by elderly retirees named "Bob" or "Mary." We have gone there to attend memorial gatherings for my brother, Peter. He died a few months earlier in a hospital near his home in France. I have spooned his ashes into the St. Croix River, as he had requested. All of this is surely enough to keep me from my writing, from making an ending. My life seems littered with endings. Friends get ill and don't come out to visit as they used to. They sell their big homes and downsize. They move away to be nearer their adult children. Some even die.

The summer flurry abates and I find myself reflecting on other endings in my life. There have been many. The end of life in England, leaving father and family, the abrupt departure from Tennessee. Did Peter and I have time for a final visit to our Florida beach before we said goodbye? Farm life in Minnesota lasted only one snow-covered, adventurous winter. I often dream that I am enclosed in a room, a small windowless space. I have arrived there through a series of doors which shut behind me. I do not feel trapped, but those doors are closed and I make no attempt to open them. My child's mind has stored many people and places behind those doors. My father seems to have had his place there. It has been best that way. Somehow I have always looked ahead to doors that open before me. I can move on. Forgetting has its uses.

How do I write this, the great reunion between my father and myself? What was it like when you first saw him? What did you think? What did you feel? But first let's take time for logistics, the narrative, the journey itself.

It is September, 1959. I have been married for several weeks. I am 21 years old. I wear a gold wedding band on the third finger of my left hand. It is tucked behind my engagement ring, a modest diamond, an heirloom from my husband's family. My hair is dark brown, eyes hazel. I am not tall but not too short. I am slim but not thin. I have been blessed with good looks, but I am not vain. I imagine myself to be fairly ordinary. I wear a traditional bridal gown on my wedding day, white taffeta, with a lace train and an inset lace panel above my breasts. Long, hot, tight fitting pointed sleeves. T and I marry in the Church of St. John the Evangelist on Portland Avenue in St. Paul, Minnesota, on the 29th day of August, 1959. The church is a few doors down from #514 where my mother, my brother and I had lived after our arrival from the Bethel farm in the spring of 1943. Bud, my stepfather, walks me down the aisle, to the strains of the "Trumpet Voluntary." The church is full.

My husband's parents and siblings, as well as many friends, are here from "The East, " a land of culture, the Ivy League, Harvard, Yale, Princeton, the Social Register. Here in our Midwestern social circles, we understand the code. Local offerings do not quite measure up, though you are not meant to say so. And here I am, evacuee child once homeless in war, joining the club. My Radcliffe education and my marriage unlock the doors.

The temperature is a steamy 95 degrees. My acquired and loving grandparents loan their house on Kenwood Parkway in St. Paul for our wedding reception. My Granny Vaughan, my father's mother, is just a one curry story to me. Nothing more. My Grandma Dubber, my maternal grandmother, showed up from England, sailing to New York on the *Queen Mary*, that very hot summer when we were eleven years old, never to be seen again. Bud's parents, Grandmother and Grandfather Stutz, easily and generously took up residence in those vacant places. They gave us seats at their table from the very first moments of our Minnesota life.

My new husband and I arrive at Minneapolis Wold Chamberlain Field for our wedding night flight to New York, only to discover that it has been cancelled. We finally get out on a coach cargo flight at 2.00 a.m., seated next to an aircraft engine in transport. The flight attendants give us champagne in honor of our newly-married status. We manage to find the family car left for us at La Guardia airport. Finally, tired but happy, we come to rest at our honeymoon destination, the Swayze lakeside home in Sussex County, New Jersey.

After a few days, we go into New York City to my in-laws Upper East Side apartment, our temporary home. They are generous and helpful, as always, as we prepare for our trans-Atlantic journey. We will be away for two years, living in Oxford where T will study. Paddy has duplicated her own trip, booking us in Cabin Class on the "S.S. United States." My twin brother, Peter, is joining us on this return voyage.

Our father is somewhere on the other side of the ocean waiting for us. But I cannot envision him, give him corporeal substance. He is a vague concept, like a ghost who inhabits the future but is soon due at the station of the present. I don't remember being particularly excited nor even very curious about seeing him. I am simply taking life one busy step at a time. The ship's passage is to be five days. Very fast, with lots to do on board. I have a new passport in my married name made out at the British Consulate in St. Paul by my mother in her official capacity as employee of the British Foreign Office. Though I am still a British subject, I make the return journey to my native land disguised as an American.

When I try to remember my arrival there, it comes to me rather like a movie that is happening to someone else. I see a young woman dressed in a well-fitting brown tweed suit. The jacket has a small fur collar. On her feet are modest high heels. Her stockings have seams. I catch her, stopped in time, as she steps off the Boat Train which has brought her to Victoria Station, London, from the docks at Southampton. Her new husband and her twin brother are here as background figures. A tall man with wavy black hair appears. He greets them all.

Move to next scene. The newly formed group arrives at a large pale yellow stucco house somewhere in South London. The man, who is the father of the twins, has driven them there. He has parked the car in the driveway next to the house. The door to the house opens when they knock or ring. A young woman appears there. She is upset because someone has moved the baby's towels and she cannot find them. She does not greet the newcomers. End of scene. I can't go any further. Nothing comes up.

Is this all, this third party remembrance? Why can't I do better, dig up some genuine feeling, a hallelujah moment of joyous discovery? I can't because I have nothing to go on. There are no relationships here. There are labels, "father," "daughter," but, on my part at least, there is no history of connection.

Here are the facts. The man is my father, Tom Vaughan. The house is on Anerley Hill in South London, in Crystal Palace. He and his wife, Esther, had bought the house earlier in the summer when they knew T, Peter, and I were coming to England. The other young woman is Esther's daughter, Gay, who now lives there with her Australian husband, Graeme, and their infant, Mark. I want more information about this day.

When my father, Tom, was 79 years old he completed his autobiography. Very long, very detailed, all his decades are laid out in nearly 300 pages. When he died at the age of 82, he left the task of editing and promotion to my cousin, Jenny, a professional writer. He hoped it was publishable. It was not. But I have it. I turn pages, wondering if he can help me. In Chapter 17, he devotes two rather brief pages to our return. He begins by giving his answer to the frequently asked question:

Paddy had kept up a desultory correspondence, sending me photographs of the children at various stages of their growth and informing me of their progress through their schools. I had taken a firm decision from the moment that I was certain that she wasn't going to return, and particularly of course when she had remarried, that I was going

to do nothing which would make the childrens' lives any more compli-
cated than they already were.

Rightly or wrongly, I came to the conclusion that nothing could be
more unsettling for them than to be constantly reminded of a strange
person five thousand miles away calling himself their father. She had a
husband helping her to bring them up; it wouldn't be fair on him either.

I can't say I ever felt very happy about thus deliberately cutting myself
off from my own children, but I consoled myself by maintaining quite
honestly that I thought it was in their own interests.

This is not news to me. It is the standard mantra, the rationalization. I
have read it before during my own efforts to help Jenny with footnotes. I
find it as devoid of feeling as my fragmented memory of our reunion day.
However, Tom is able to add his own touch to our reunion at Victoria
Station. He helps me:

It is certainly a strange experience suddenly being confronted by two
young people who exhibit not only all sorts of reminders of yourself but
also — quite unexpectedly — of all sorts of other people as well.

The first impression of them was one of shortness and, as far as Peter
was concerned, of the Dubber inheritance. But unmistakably — about her
eyes and cheekbones — Felicity was my mother all over again, and Peter's
sheathed dark eyes and general air of unpredictability revealed an inner
insecurity that reminded me of myself at his age. He had obviously taken
his semi-orphanage much harder than his sister and in that he hadn't
changed at all since he was a baby. He was still the passionate introvert,
Felicity the serene extrovert, just as they had been when I saw them off at
Euston station back in 1940.

I wonder how he can be so sure. We were only two and half years old when he
last saw us. I remind myself that he wrote this after he had known us as adults
for many years. Perhaps he is simply operating from benefit of hindsight. He
may be recreating a past of his own invention. But this explanation doesn't fit

for me.   We had lived together for nearly three years. Babies become children quickly, forming attachments to people and places with lightening speed. He was there with us and we with him. He came to know us well enough to grasp the essentials. For we are as he describes us. Somehow, over all these years, a thread of connection is still there, managing, even without nurture, to stay alive in him.   He remembers me even though I do not remember him. But it is enough to begin. Perhaps he and I can take it from here.